THE EVERYTHING KIDS' Weather Book

From tornadoes to snowstorms, puzzles, games, and facts that make weather for kids fun!

Joe Snedeker, MEd

Adams Media

New York London Toronto Sydney New Delhi

To my wife Dawn and my children Joey, Lucas, and Aleah; and to all who
don't let the noise of other's opinions drown out their own inner voice.

PUBLISHER Karen Cooper

MANAGING EDITOR, EVERYTHING® SERIES Lisa Laing

COPY CHIEF Casey Ebert

ASSISTANT PRODUCTION EDITOR Melanie Cordova

ACQUISITIONS EDITOR Kate Powers

SENIOR DEVELOPMENT EDITOR Brett Palana-Shanahan

EDITORIAL ASSISTANT Matthew Kane

EVERYTHING® SERIES COVER DESIGNER Erin Alexander

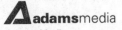

Adams Media
An Imprint of Simon & Schuster, Inc.
57 Littlefield Street
Avon, Massachusetts 02322

For information about special discounts for bulk purchases, please contact Simon & Schuster Special Sales at 1-866-506-1949 or business@simonandschuster.com.

The Simon & Schuster Speakers Bureau can bring authors to your live event. For more information or to book an event contact the Simon & Schuster Speakers Bureau at 1-866-248-3049 or visit our website at www.simonspeakers.com.

Interior illustrations by Kurt Dolber.
Puzzles by Beth Blair.

Manufactured in the United States of America

Printed by LSC Communications, Harrisonburg, VA, U.S.A.

10   9
October 2017

ISBN 978-1-4405-5036-2
ISBN 978-1-4405-5037-9 (ebook)

Visit the entire Everything® series at *www.everything.com*

Dear Parents and Teachers,

Admit it: You, too, are curious about the weather. Who isn't? It's one of the few things that affects nearly everything and everyone and is a constant topic of conversation. The local and national news refer to it every day, and it even has its very own cable channel. But how much do you really know about the weather?

What is a cold front? How high are clouds? Why is the sky blue? How fast does the jet stream move? What causes the seasons to change? What is a barometer? If you deal with children, you're going to get many of those questions or similar ones about the weather. How will you respond? As a television meteorologist, former high school science teacher, college meteorology instructor, and parent of three children under the age of eleven, I can tell you this—everyone is interested in the science of weather. Everyone!

One of my favorite quotes goes something like this: "Only a fool makes something more difficult than it has to be." We all know people who can take a subject and make it more complex, confusing, and—dare I say—more boring than it has to be. The goal of this book is to do just the opposite: take a complex science like meteorology and make it fun, understandable, and very readable for young children. With the use of everyday examples, colorful and imaginative words, images, pictures, charts, games, and puzzles, the science of meteorology will come alive for your young reader!

So go ahead, let the science of weather come alive for your readers as they page through the chapters of this book. But beware, you may find yourself peeking into the book when your children are not around just to find out how weather works. Good luck and read on!

—Joe Snedeker

Contents

Introduction

Give this a try. Right now, start swinging your arms around. Faster! What do you feel? Silly? Tired? Sore? Don't forget about what else you're feeling—air! You can feel it swirling and flowing over and around your arms. That is Earth's atmosphere. Your atmosphere! The air around you and everything in your world is the atmosphere. The study of the atmosphere and how it produces our day-to-day weather is called *meteorology*. Now stop swinging.

Nearly everyone and everything is affected by the weather and the movement and interaction of gasses swirling around our planet. Your school, your parents, the mountains in the distance, and the food in your refrigerator—they're all influenced and changed by the weather. Perhaps you've wondered why the air around you produces everything from devastating tornadoes to calm, warm, sunny days at the beach. In *The Everything® Kids' Weather Book*, you'll find out everything you've always wanted to know about our weather, from the reason the sky is blue to how thunderstorms form and fill the sky with white-hot lightning and ear-pounding thunder!

This book is loaded with the information you need to understand and even forecast the weather. You'll find out exactly what the air around you is made up of (you're breathing it in right now; you should definitely know what's in it) and why it often gathers and swirls into school-canceling snowstorms. You'll get to know and understand cloud types, cold fronts, hurricanes, and jet stream winds. With some simple supplies from your house, you'll be able to start building your own home weather station and begin to truly understand just how our weather works. Beware; you may end up becoming a true master of air, a sultan of skies, or better yet, one who truly understands and studies weather—a meteorologist. So start swinging your arms again, this time from excitement. As Benjamin Franklin put it, "Some people are weatherwise, but most are otherwise."

CHAPTER 1

Weather, Weather Everywhere?

Words to Know

meteorologist

A meteorologist is a scientist who studies the earth's atmosphere and weather. Weather forecasters may not be meteorologists. Many television stations have weather forecasters who just talk about and broadcast the weather. Meteorologists have science degrees from a college or university.

Try This

NAME THE RAIN

Precipitation is moisture that falls from the air to the ground. Try and name as many forms of precipitation as you can. Get started with rain and snow. There are at least three others.

WHAT IS WEATHER?

Did you know there are places on Earth where it hasn't rained in hundreds of years? Would you say that they have weather? There are other places on this planet where it rains almost every day! Do they have more weather? What about your weather? Check outside right now; see what it is doing out there. That is weather. It's now, it's happening, and it's an exciting and ever-changing science. It is the realm of a meteorologist, a person who studies the weather.

Between you reading this book and the cold, dark emptiness of space, there are layers of stuff. A lot of stuff! That stuff is *air*. It rises up, sinks, and swirls around. In places it moves over 300 miles per hour, and in other spots it's perfectly still. Some spots on the earth are getting drenched with rain at this moment, while other locations are in the middle of a dry, sand-blasting dust storm. It's all weather.

The air around the earth is called the *atmosphere*. What the atmosphere is doing and how it acts is referred to as the weather. Things like temperature, wind, clouds, humidity, and precipitation all help describe the weather. It is always changing, and no two spots have exactly the same weather conditions on any given time on the planet.

There is an end to Earth's weather, and it is only about an hour's car drive away!

It's a place not too far away from you, probably closer than the mall or your favorite amusement park. If you could get into a car and drive it straight up into the sky, after about an hour of traveling, or about 50 miles, the air would soon run out. You would be in space! With practically no air, wind, rain, or cloudy skies, it's a place of no weather.

HOW EARTH GOT ITS AIR

Reach out for some air and push it in your face. Blow some of that all-natural air right into the person next to you. Picture in your mind a Tyrannosaurus rex chasing a triceratops at top speed gasping for air as they run through a foggy river valley. Much of the air that was in their lungs and in that fog is still around today, perhaps flowing into your nostrils right now! Yes, air is recycled. It's been here on Earth a long, long time.

All that air, for millions and million of years? Actually, Earth's atmosphere is over four and a half billion years old! That's the number 45 with 8 zeros after it! If we were to go back to the beginning of the earth, long before the time of the dinosaurs, and fly above the young Earth, you wouldn't be looking at the bright blue and white marble you see today. Earth's atmosphere has changed much over time, and so has its weather.

When Earth was forming, its surface was a hot, lava-filled, steamy, and lifeless place very different from today. Chunks of rocks and ice from space were constantly smashing into it as it formed, adding to it and changing it with every collision. Large volcanoes erupted and burped out gases from the inside in a process known as *outgassing*. In much the same way that gravity pulls you back to the surface when you jump, Earth's gravity pulled many of these gases back to the surface of the baby planet Earth. Air was sticking to the surface, and its first atmosphere was starting to form! The weather and air then were still very different from today.

FUN FACT
Mini-Earth

If the earth were shrunken down to the size of a desk globe, the thickness of the atmosphere and all the weather would be thinner than the edge of a coin. All weather, clouds, storms, and precipitation occur in the thickness of that coin.

STRAW SCIENCE

You've done it before, now you can do it in the name of science. With your family, blow air through a straw into a drinking glass half filled with water. The bubbles of air that come out of the water are outgassing, in the same way that air bubbled out of Earth's insides billions of years ago! That air helped form the atmosphere. Bubble away!

No Air to Breathe?

Have you ever noticed the cloud of moisture that forms from your breath on a cold day? The same thing happened to Earth as it continued to cool off over time. The warm breath of volcanic eruptions cooled off in the air, producing steam and clouds of moisture that led to Earth's first rain storms. Rain washed off the land and river water collected into large pools, forming Earth's first oceans. Going back to this time you might just recognize your home planet, with oceans separating the land, puffy clouds, and storms spinning out rain from the equator to the North Pole and South Pole. There were many things that were different then. There was no life on the planet and no oxygen to breath. The air was poisonous, and the temperature was much warmer than today.

About 4 billion years ago, the first signs of life on the planet were just getting started. Microscopic simple life forms, still around today and known as bacteria, started to change the atmosphere in new ways. These little guys didn't need oxygen to live, but they gave it off as they grew and multiplied in the sun-filled oceans. With its new life, Earth continued to change, cool, settle down, and fill with oxygen. The planet grew more and more life over long periods of time, leading to big breathers like you. Take a deep breath; we've come a long way!

Tiny Air Makers

Bacteria are very tiny single-celled creatures. Hundreds of bacteria can fit in the dot at the end of this sentence. Bacteria have been found everywhere, from the highest mountain to the deepest part of the sea. There are billions of bacteria living on and in your body producing and giving off different gasses.

Watch the Weather

When people spent much of their lives outside, the weather was very important! Everyone watched for patterns to help predict the weather. Then they made up rhymes to help remember the patterns.

Rearrange the letters into familiar words. The definitions will give you hints. When you are done, put the numbered letters in the correct places to complete the weather rhyme!

W E _ _ _ O _ N _ S
_6_ 1 _ 2 _ 3 4 _ 5

_ R A _ E _ _ F _ R
6 _ 7 _ 8 _ 9

_ N D _ _ _ I _ E,
10 _ 11 _ 12 _ 13

_ T _ R _ Y _ D _ _
14 15 16 17 18

_ I L _ A R _ _ E.
19 20 21 22 23

Places to bake cakes

VSENO

— — — —
   23   2   14

The opposite of quiet

ODUL

— — — —
8   15   4   12

Bend gently back and forth

WASY

— — — —
3   19   9   18

A bride's long white headdress

IVEL

— — — —
7   22   20

Prize given to the winner

DAARW

— — — — —
10   11   17   21   5

Adding and subtracting

ATMH

— — — —
16   13   6   1

11

WHAT IS AIR?

FUN FACT

Elements of Everything!

There are 118 different types of elements, but only 98 exist naturally on our world. Elements are made up of a certain type of atom. Hydrogen is the simplest type of atom and the most common one in the universe. It's even one of the most common types making up your body!

FUN FACT

Water: Two Ears and a Head!

A water molecule is shaped just like the head of Mickey Mouse. The face of Mickey would represent the oxygen atom, while the two ears on each side are the hydrogen atoms. Billions of these heads make up the smallest drop of water!

You can feel it by swinging your arms and see it as a force that can cause a flag to flap, but what exactly is air? You've probably learned by now that nearly everything is made up of tiny little particles way too small to be seen by your eyes, called atoms. These tiny particles make up everything, from coat hangers to ponies, from stars to cars. Everything, yes even you! So they must make up our air, too.

There are many different types of atoms. Gold, oxygen, iron, and hydrogen are the names of a few atoms you may have heard or read about. Just like letters in the alphabet can be grouped in different ways to make different words, atoms can group in many ways to make many different types of stuff, like air! Compounds and molecules are the names given to atoms that join together to make different kinds of stuff. Two hydrogen atoms and one oxygen atom can group together to make a molecule of water . . . H_2O. Yes, the water you drink is a glass full of atoms!

So what are the atoms and molecules in the air between your eyes and this book? What is it you are breathing in? What is it that is blowing the leaves across the road? Atoms of nitrogen and oxygen make up most of the air, over 99 percent. The rest of the air is a mix of many different types of atoms and molecules, all bouncing around like Ping-Pong balls in the form of a gas. As a gas, the molecules are invisible. When atoms and molecules get closer together and pack tight, they are no longer a gas but exist in the form of a solid or a liquid and can be seen.

Water is a special molecule that can exist as a solid, liquid, or gas in the air. Water is only a tiny part of all the molecules of air, but it's a big, big part of all weather. Water helps form what we think of as weather. Weather conditions like snow, rain, cloudy skies, high humidity, and thunderstorms are all from the action of water molecules! Without water in the air, weather as we know it would not exist!

A METEOROLOGIST'S PLAYGROUND

There is more to the earth's atmosphere and meteorology than just air! It's what air does that makes weather. From where you are sitting to outer space above you, there is so much going on that meteorologists divide up the air into different sections as shown here.

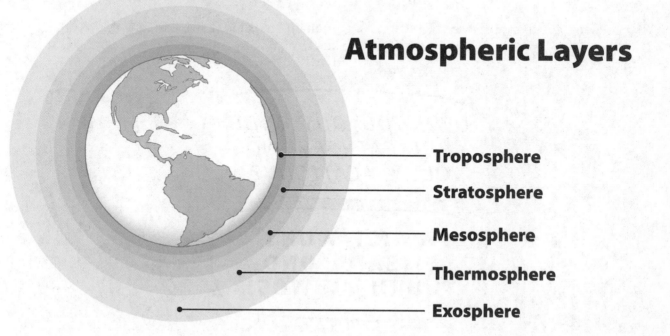

Atmospheric Layers

- **Troposphere**
- **Stratosphere**
- **Mesosphere**
- **Thermosphere**
- **Exosphere**

Temperatures usually drop about 20°F for every mile you go up into Earth's first layer, the *troposphere*. Because of this, even in the summer the tops of mountains can be very cold and snow covered. Airplanes and jets flying just a few miles above the ground also experience temperatures that are usually near or below zero.

Just as there are different zones and parts of a playground, Earth's atmosphere is divided up into separate areas, each with its own characteristics. Beginning at the bottom, there is the troposphere. That's where you are now. All the day-to-day weather and clouds occur in this layer. It surrounds all of the cities as well as the deepest valleys and highest mountains. When you see a high-flying jet above your head, it's probably flying near the top of the troposphere, about 7 miles up.

Above the troposphere, the air is very, very thin, and temperatures are very cold. In this second layer, known as the *stratosphere*, there's not even enough air to breathe or for weather as you know it to occur. But the stratosphere con-

Chit Chat

People spend a lot of time talking about the weather! Break the First to Last, and the Vowel Switch codes to learn the two halves of this silly conversation.

OWH IDD OUY INDF HET EATHERW NO OURY ACATIONV?

A JIST WUNT EITSADU OND THURU AT WOS!

tains a layer of air that most life on Earth depends on: the ozone layer. There, dangerous rays from the sun are blocked out and prevented from reaching life on the surface. Without the ozone layer, sunburns would be so bad that most life would die from the intense sunlight.

Above the stratosphere are the *mesosphere* and *thermosphere*. In these zones it's almost spacelike, with hardly any air and an eerie blackness to the sky, but there is still some activity. Have you ever seen a shooting star at night? Shooting stars are really small pieces of rock and space dust burning up at the top of the atmosphere. Yes, way up there, over 50 miles up, there is still SOME air. After that, the air slowly disappears and turns into outer space!

Glowing Lights from Above?

Have you ever heard of the northern lights? Sometimes the top of Earth's atmosphere glows like a neon light! Way up there in the thermosphere and beyond, atoms still float around on the edge of air and space. When light from the sun hits these atoms, they break up and become active. During certain years, when the sun is more active, more energy hits the atoms at the top of the atmosphere. The atoms begin to give off light as a result of all of the sun's added energy. The night sky can light up in colors of blue, green, orange, yellow, and pink in a beautiful display called the northern lights or aurora borealis. They are often seen near the North and South Poles of Earth when the nights are very long!

Try This

NORTHERN LIGHTS IN YOUR BEDROOM!

Make your own northern lights. In a dark room with no light, try rubbing a balloon on your pajamas or blankets under the covers. You may be able to see brief bursts of light produced as the balloon and material rub against each other, disturbing the atoms. In a way, that's what happens in the upper atmosphere as sunlight interacts with atoms.

WEATHER ON OTHER PLANETS

Once you leave Earth's atmosphere, you're in space! It's cold, it's dark, and there is no air. To find more air outside of Earth's atmosphere, you'd have to travel to another planet. Just think, in our solar system there are seven other planets, each with some air wrapped around it. Each of these planets has its own type of air and weather that is very different from what you are used to on Earth. Some of the stars you see in the sky at night are not stars but planets. That dot you see in the sky at night may actually be air and weather on another world. What could it be like there? Scientists have studied the planets with telescopes and special spacecraft. Many interesting things and strange weather have been found on many of them.

Dust storms, tornadoes, sunny skies, lightning, and volcanoes as big as the state of Texas have all been discovered on other worlds in our solar system. Temperatures were so hot and the air was so heavy that the spacecraft that were sent to study some of these worlds were crushed like soda cans. In other places, it's so cold there are oceans of solid ice. Of all the planets, only two, Mars and Venus, are similar to Earth, but their weather and air are very different from ours.

Venus has thick, poisonous clouds and temperatures that get hotter than a turkey baking in an oven, as heat is trapped by an atmosphere with too much air. Mars has temperatures that are often colder than Antarctica and an atmosphere so thin that if you were sent there without a space suit, most of the blood and fluids in your body would turn to gas while you froze solid! The planet closest to the sun, Mercury, has almost no air and skies as black as ink in the middle of the day, just like on our moon.

MORNING STAR!

The planet Venus is known as the morning star. It is called the morning star because it is often seen just before sunrise in the eastern sky. Try getting up some morning before sunrise and looking to the east to see the planet Venus. You can't miss it; it'll be the brightest-looking star. Think about the poisonous clouds and 800°F weather there. Then have some breakfast!

The big outer planets like Jupiter, Saturn, Uranus, and Neptune are mostly all atmosphere. They have too much air and no ground to stand on! Jupiter has had a swirling storm system the size of three Earths in its clouds for more than 400 years! Ever see a picture of Jupiter and its big red spot? That red spot is the swirling storm system. The extreme pressure, temperatures, and violent conditions on all of these worlds make Earth and its air even sweeter. From outer space, Earth looks calm, cool, blue, and white—inviting compared to other places in our solar system. Look outside a window and say it . . . HOME SWEET HOME!

EARTH'S CHANGING WEATHER AND GLOBAL WARMING

Do you remember Earth's age from earlier in this chapter? It's over four and a half billion years old! That's the number 45 with 8 zeros after it! That is a long, long, long time! Just like people grow and change over time, Earth's atmosphere and weather have changed drastically from warmer to colder periods many times. In the past, the earth's surface has been nearly frozen solid like a snow cone and other times completely ice free and very warm and tropical.

An example of this includes the time when dinosaurs walked the planet. During part of the time of the dinosaurs (over 65 million years ago), our planet was much different than it is now, with an atmosphere filled with more carbon dioxide and warmer temperatures. As recently as just fifteen thousand years ago, opposite conditions occurred,

Sunny Sky, Cloudy Sky

The weather can change from minute to minute! See if you can make a path through this maze alternating cloudy skies with sunny skies, ending with a sunny day. Here are the rules: You can travel side to side or up and down, but not diagonally. If you come to a lightning storm, you are going the wrong way.

with temperatures much colder than they are now. During that time thick ice sheets and mountains of snow covered what is now much of the northern part of the United States, Europe, and Asia. That was a time known as the Ice Age. Imagine solid ice and snow extending from the North Pole all the way to what is now New York City. It happened!

It now seems that our weather is changing again. This time, the changes might be because of human activities. Recently, our modern world has been using and burning fossil fuels in great amounts. Fossil fuels are nonrenewable resources like coal, oil, and gas that have been stored in the earth for millions of years. Today we use these fuels to power our cars, planes, factories, and cities. Fossil fuels are used to make electricity that light up your home and give your television and computers the energy they need. Burning these fuels, however, often adds pollution and carbon dioxide to our air.

Remember what is happening on the planet Venus? Gasses like carbon dioxide help to trap heat in, acting like a blanket, which can slowly warm a planet. Over the last few decades, meteorologists have measured an increase in Earth's temperatures. If this weather warm-up continues, our planet may change in ways that could affect the polar ice caps, the world's ocean levels, and weather patterns. Many living things on the planet would have to adjust to a new set of weather patterns in a very short amount of time. Maybe too short a time!

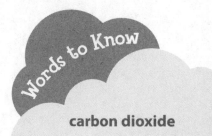

Words to Know

carbon dioxide

Carbon dioxide is one of the most common elements on earth. It is made up of only three atoms, one carbon atom and two oxygen atoms. Every time you breathe out you release carbon dioxide. However, if the air has large quantities of carbon dioxide, it can be toxic.

WHICH ONE ?

Our modern world needs energy. Which of the following ways of getting energy adds carbon dioxide and pollution to the atmosphere and may also be contributing to global warming?

1. Solar energy
2. Wind turbines
3. Burning coal
4. Nuclear energy

3. Burning coal

CHAPTER 2

Under Pressure

Really, Really Heavy Air!

Air pressure on the planet Venus is almost 100 times greater than air pressure on Earth. Russian spacecraft sent to Venus were crushed in less than an hour by the heavy air.

AIR HAS WEIGHT

Do you remember the last time you stepped on a scale? How much did you weigh? What is weight? Since you are made of stuff, gravity pulls you downward. The more stuff you are made of, the more gravity can pull you down. A car weighs more than a pencil because a car has more stuff than a pencil for gravity to pull on. As you found out in Chapter 1, air is stuff. Air is made up of atoms, molecules, and compounds that get pulled down by Earth's gravity. Air is held to the ground by gravity, just like a pencil, a car, and yourself. All that air and all that gravity result in a lot of pressure!

AIR: HEAVIER THAN AN ELEPHANT, LIGHTER THAN A FEATHER

Have you ever gone bowling? Imagine the weight of that bowling ball in your hand as you carry it to the bowling lane. Now imagine holding in your hand a tube of air about the size of a garden hose that goes straight up into the sky over 50 miles! Put your hand out and imagine it. How much do you think that weighs? Heavier than a bowling ball? It's only a small tube of air, right?

The weight of that imaginary tube would be about 15 pounds! If you were to try and hold up about twenty of those long tubes of air in your hand it would weigh nearly 300 pounds! That's almost like holding a baby elephant in the palm of your hand. Extend your hand out again and feel over 300 pounds of air pushing down on it. I bet you don't feel a thing. It's as light as a feather. How could this be?

The force of weight of the air and its molecules is called *air pressure*. But air pressure does not just push down from above; it squeezes in from all directions. So in your hand you are not only holding tubes of air on the up side of your hand but the "push" of air molecules from the side, bottom, and all over your hand. With all those forces working together all over your hand, you feel nothing. That's why when you hold out your hand it seems like there is no air pressure. But it is there, pushing on all sides, and there are a few ways you can have the invisible force of air pressure do some work!

Try putting the palm of your hand over your mouth. Make a tight seal with your lips and start sucking inward. You think you're sucking the skin of your hand into your mouth, right? Wrong! What you've done is removed the air pressure from that part of your hand touching your mouth, and now the atmospheric pressure and air from the other side of your hand is pushing in, with the equal weight of a bowling ball! Alright, stop sucking! Try this to feel more of its force. Ask your parents for an empty plastic soda bottle. With your mouth, suck out the air from the open end of the bottle and watch the plastic collapse inward. Once you sucked out the air from inside of the bottle, the atmosphere outside of the bottle was able to push in and crushed the bottle with its air pressure and weight. Air is heavy!

MORE STRAW SCIENCE!

Place a straw into a glass of water and suck some of the water up into the straw. Now, with your finger, block off the opening of the straw end that was in your mouth. Notice how the water stays in the straw! Why? Since you're blocking the opening at the top with your finger, the only place air pressure can get into the straw is from the bottom, so it holds up the water in the straw. Once you let air back in over your finger, the water drops out of the straw as air pressure pulls it down.

Rhyme Time

In the time before cars, electricity, and television, people spent much of their lives outside. For these people, weather was very important! Everyone watched for patterns to help predict the weather. Then they made up rhymes to help remember these patterns.

    An old-fashioned weather rhyme has been put into a puzzle grid and cut into pieces. Match the pattern of black squares, and figure out where each piece goes. Then write the letters into the empty grid.

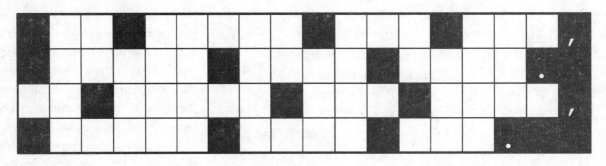

AIR MOVES, JUST WATCH THE WIND

Air pressure exists all over the earth's surface, but it changes a little bit from place to place and day to day. Yes, air can weigh a little more today than it did yesterday. Today there may be more air over New York and less in Paris, or less over your house and more over your grandmother's just a few miles away. It's always changing, and those differences have a major affect on your weather. You can feel it in the wind!

Imagine a balloon filled with air. What happens when that balloon gets a tiny hole in it? The air flows out of the balloon, from a place where there is more air (inside the balloon) to a place where there is less air (outside of the balloon). The result is more than a deflated balloon, it's the creation of *wind*. Yes, pressure differences make the air move. Moving air is WIND! Air pressure differences cause the wind to blow. The greater the difference in air pressure, the faster the wind blows!

Now the big question is, why does air pressure change from place to place and day to day all over the earth? Air pressure is changed by many factors and conditions across the planet. Remember, you are living on a spinning ball of water, rock, and ice heated by the sun, millions of miles away. That heat is not spread equally over the surface of the earth. Some places get warmer, others colder. The differences in heat, along with the shape of the earth's surface and the spinning of the planet all form the changing pattern of air pressure and wind. As a matter of fact, the pressure around you reading this book has changed from the time you started this paragraph! If you stepped outside right now, you would feel those changes in the air that is moving, making wind. Amazing!

FUN FACT

Which Way Did the Wind Go?

Wind direction is always given in the direction that the air is coming from. An east wind means that air is moving from the east to the west. The most common wind direction in the United States is a west wind. That is, air is moving from the west to the east.

MEASURING THE WEIGHT OF THE AIR

FUN FACT

What's in a Name?

The word *barometer* comes from the Greek word *baros*, meaning "weight."

Knowing how much the air weighs from place to place is very important in forecasting and understanding the weather. Meteorologists use air pressure patterns and maps to understand where storm centers are, where they're going, and how fast they will move. All over the planet are special instruments used to measure air pressure, or how heavy the air is, and if it's changing its weight. These instruments are called *barometers*. You may even have one hanging on the wall in your house or school. They're everywhere!

Think of a barometer like a scale that is used to measure your weight. If a bigger person steps on a scale, the reading will be higher than if someone who is tiny stepped on the scale. In the same way, when the air is heavy, or higher in pressure, the barometer will display a higher reading. Light air will be displayed as a low reading on a barometer, showing lower air pressure. There are two main types of air scales, or barometers: aneroid and mercury.

Mercury barometers use mercury, which is a special metal that exists naturally at room temperature as a liquid, like water, but is much heavier. On this instrument, mercury is sealed in a glass tube and placed like a straw into an open container of more mercury. When the air pressure pushes down onto the mercury in the container, it forces it up the glass tube! Heavy air with great air pressure pushes the mercury higher in the tube than lighter air. The level of the mercury in the tube then displays the air pressure! On average, the mercury in the tube will rise to a height of about 30 inches. Perhaps you've heard a meteorologist report the barometer as a reading of 30 inches. Now you know why!

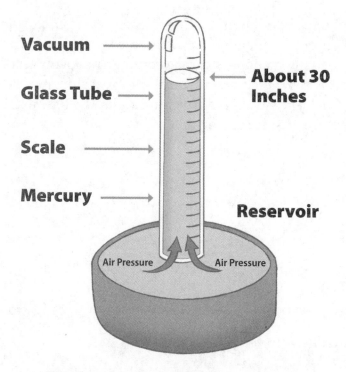

Vacuum

Glass Tube

Scale

Mercury

About 30 Inches

Reservoir

Air Pressure Air Pressure

Mercury Barometer

An aneroid barometer usually shows air pressure with a pointer displayed on a round dial like you would see on a clock. The pointer is connected to a special small metal box inside the instrument called a vacuum chamber. The vacuum chamber is like a little box, only most of the air has been sucked out of it. In a way, it's like conditions in space, or around our moon, with very little or no molecules of air. When the air outside the aneroid barometer gets heavier or greater in pressure, the little box gets squeezed in. When the air pressure outside the barometer gets lighter, or has less pressure, the little box expands outward. The movements of the little vacuum box are connected to a pointer that shows the air pressure.

Try This

HOMEMADE BAROMETER

Make a barometer. All you need is a large rubber balloon, an elastic band, and a can or jar and other simple supplies. With help from an adult, cut the open end of the balloon off. Stretch the remaining large piece of rubber over the open end of a jar or can until it makes a tight, flat surface covering the entire opening. Secure the rubber over the can or jar with an elastic band. Attach a straw to the center of the rubber with white glue (hot glue may cause the balloon to melt) so that it hangs over the can or jar like a pointer. It's done! When air pressure increases, it will push down on the rubber and the straw pointer will point up. When air pressure decreases, the rubber will expand outward (bulge) and the straw pointer will point down. You can monitor air pressure changes right in your house. Leave your barometer inside a dry room with little change in temperature.

F U N F A C T

Lightest Air Ever?

One of the lowest barometer readings recorded was 26.18 inches of mercury near the center of Hurricane Gilbert in the Atlantic Ocean in 1988. The winds blew over 175 miles per hour because the air pressure was so low!

Watching a barometer reading change is very important in weather forecasting. When the barometer reading starts to fall, it usually means a storm is coming or a low-pressure area is nearby. When a barometer reading goes up, it usually means dry weather and sunshine are in the forecast, or a high-pressure area is moving in!

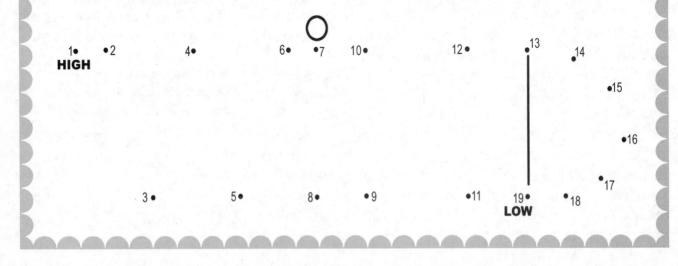

High to Low

Something happens when air moves from an area of HIGH pressure to an area of LOW pressure. Connect the dots to see what it is. You can connect the dots in order from high to low, or backwards from low to high. Either way, the result is the same!

THE HIGHS AND LOWS OF WEATHER MAPS

Alright, you now know all about air pressure! Now it's time for you to use that information and have fun using weather maps. Let's say at this moment meteorologists across the entire United States are all reading their barometers. You can then plot the readings of the barometers on a map, just like the following one. Remember, the barometer readings are given in numbers that are in inches of mercury.

Look at all of the barometer readings and find the highest and lowest pressure. Now, think about this. Have you ever seen a weather map on television or in the paper with the

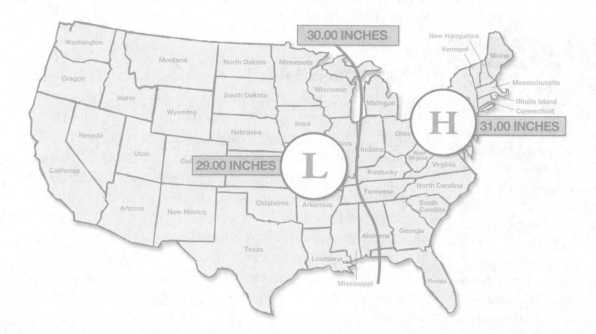

Try This

BAROMETER DIARY!

Write down the barometer reading that you get from your local weather forecast. Keep a log of all the readings and watch how the barometer changes with your weather. You can also watch how areas of high and low pressure on weather maps change the barometer readings and weather where you live.

F U N F A C T

clockwise and counterclockwise

Air and wind usually form a spinning pattern around areas of high and low pressure. Around a high-pressure area, the wind moves clockwise, or in the direction of the hands on a clock. Around a low-pressure area, the wind moves counterclockwise, or in the opposite direction as the hands on a clock. Meteorologists often use these terms, and they are opposite in the Northern Hemisphere compared to the Southern Hemisphere.

letters *H* or *L* on the map? They represent areas of high and low pressure. Look at your map again and you will find an area of low pressure near the center of the map in the state of Missouri. The pressure there is only about 29.00 inches of mercury. Farther east near Pennsylvania, the pressure is the greatest at about 31.00 inches of mercury. You are now reading a weather map and understanding why there are areas of high and low pressure on it!

Even more exciting is just what those highs and lows mean for weather forecasters. In an area of low pressure, the air is very light and rises upward into the sky. Rising air cools, usually forming clouds, precipitation, and windy conditions. Hurricanes, cyclones, and nor'easters are examples of low-pressure areas. In an area of high pressure, the air is heavy and sinks downward toward the ground. Near an area of high pressure, air does not rise up and cool, so clouds and precipitation usually do not form. High-pressure areas are usually areas of clear skies, light winds, and sunshine during the day!

Watch Them Spin

Remember what happens if you put a small hole in a balloon? Air moves out from the balloon because it is under high pressure. The same thing happens to high- and low-pressure areas in weather. Air moves as wind out from a high-pressure system and into a low-pressure system. Low-pressure systems usually produce rain, snow, and clouds, but they also suck air into themselves like a big vacuum cleaner. Because of the spinning of the earth, the wind and air circulate inward toward the center, forming a whirlpool-like pattern. When you see a hurricane or cyclone, it often forms into a large spinning area of clouds shaped like a pinwheel or water spinning in a flushed toilet. The "eye" of a

Blow Hard

Wind is a very useful type of weather. It can be used to dry clothes, fly kites, and sail boats. There is another way to use wind that is particularly important in this day and age. Break the fraction code to find out what it is!

Look at the fraction below each blank. Pick the shape that shows that fraction, using these rules: the white part of each shape is empty; the shaded part of each shape is full. Write the letter of that shape on the line.

___ ___ ___ D C ___ ___ ___ ___ R ___ ___ H ___
$\frac{1}{4}$ $\frac{2}{6}$ $\frac{1}{3}$ $\frac{1}{2}$ $\frac{1}{3}$ $\frac{2}{4}$ $\frac{2}{5}$ $\frac{1}{3}$ $\frac{2}{4}$ $\frac{2}{3}$

B L ___ D ___ S ___ F H ___ G H- ___ ___ C H
   $\frac{1}{2}$ $\frac{2}{3}$ $\frac{3}{6}$ $\frac{2}{6}$ $\frac{2}{4}$ $\frac{2}{3}$

___ ___ ___ D ___ ___ R B ___ ___ ___ S ___ ___
$\frac{1}{4}$ $\frac{2}{6}$ $\frac{1}{3}$ $\frac{2}{4}$ $\frac{2}{5}$ $\frac{2}{6}$ $\frac{1}{3}$ $\frac{2}{3}$ $\frac{2}{4}$ $\frac{3}{6}$

M ___ K ___ ___ L ___ C ___ R ___ C ___ ___ Y.
  $\frac{1}{2}$ $\frac{2}{3}$ $\frac{2}{3}$ $\frac{2}{3}$ $\frac{2}{4}$ $\frac{2}{6}$ $\frac{2}{6}$ $\frac{2}{4}$

A

T

O

I

W

N

E

U

31

hurricane is located in the center of large spinning area of low pressure.

Next time you see a weather map on television, in the newspaper, or on a computer, look for the areas of high and low pressure. Think about the weather that is happening near these areas. Meteorologists use barometers to locate areas of high and low pressure and where they might move. As the high- and low-pressure areas move across the country, they change the weight of the air and weather near them. You can build a barometer, watch the weather maps, and do the same thing a meteorologist does, even forecast the weather for your town.

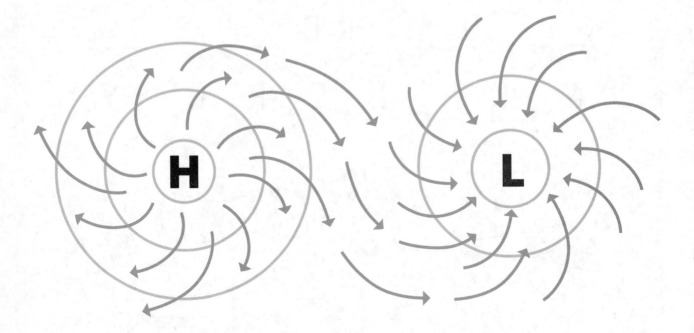

High and Low Pressure

Wacky Weather

Many people confuse weather with climate. Are they the same or not? Put the numbered words or letter groups in the correct spaces to find the silly answer to this question!

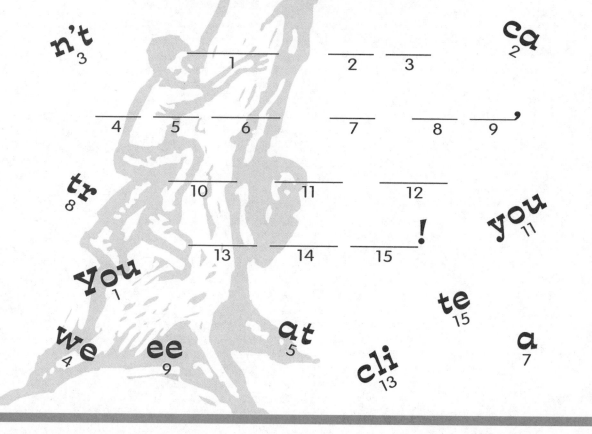

can
12

ma
14

but
10

her
6

What's the difference between weather and climate?

n't
3

ca
2

___ ___ ___
1   2   3

___ ___ ___ ___ ___ ___ ,
4   5   6   7   8   9

tr
8

___ ___ ___
10   11   12

you
11

___ ___ ___ !
13   14   15

you
1

te
15

we
4

ee
9

at
5

cli
13

a
7

33

CHAPTER 3

Water in the Air and Clouds in the Sky

F U N F A C T

Water Is Special

Water is the only compound that commonly exists in three forms on Earth. Water takes the form of a solid as ice, a liquid as water, and a gas as vapor in the air. As you read this, there is probably ice in your refrigerator, liquid water near your sink, and invisible water vapor in the air around you. No other substance exists like that in all three forms.

Words to Know

evaporation

The physical change when water moves from a liquid to a gas.

All in a Drop of Water!

In a single drop of water there are about 300,000,000,000,000,000,000 water molecules! Picture in your mind billions and billions of them in a tiny drop of water!

HOW WATER CHANGES FORM

How many different weather terms can you think of that are all made from the same stuff—*water*? Here are a few: clouds, fog, dew, ice, snow, frost, sleet, hail, mist, rain, and humidity. Water can change form over and over again, switching from misty drops of dew to cold cubes of ice, all in a day! In many ways, water is recyclable!

Water's Magic Act

Why does water change form in so many ways? Water changes forms depending of what is acting on it. The two things that are always acting on water are—yes, you guessed it—temperature and air pressure. Think of water molecules as tiny little Ping-Pong balls, millions and millions of them, all over the place. When the temperature goes up, imagine those little Ping-Pong balls getting more active, moving faster, colliding with each other, and bouncing from place to place. What holds them in place is the pressure of the air around them, squeezing them together and holding them close. When the air pressure or temperature changes, the Ping-Pong balls change, too.

So just what do water molecules do when they change form? When water is in a solid form, like an ice cube, the Ping-Pong balls (water molecules) are close together, locked tight and not moving all that much. If the temperature goes up, the Ping-Pong balls start moving around and jumping loose, hitting each other, resulting in a change into what we see as liquid water. The ice cube would be melting! If the temperature goes up even more, the little Ping-Pong balls would bounce around faster, cut loose, and spread themselves far apart, a change known as *evaporation*. You've probably seen this happen over a pot of boiling water. In this example, water went from a solid to a liquid to a gas. It's like a magic act!

Because of water's magic, it is always changing form and putting on a new show. Puddles evaporate and later turn into clouds. Clouds can then produce rain that then falls back to the earth, forming a new puddle. Ice and snow at the top of the Himalaya Mountains may end up as some of the water molecules that are boiling out of a pot of pasta over a hot stove in your kitchen. The process of water recycling itself over the earth's surface in many different forms is known as the water cycle. Without the water cycle there would be no rain, snow, clouds, or partly sunny day. No weather!

Try This

MAGIC DROPS OF WATER

With an adult, place a small drop of water on two or three different substances in and around your house. If it's warm outside, place a drop on your sidewalk. Place another drop on a desk top. Place a third drop on something cooler, like a metal object. Guess which drop will evaporate first. Watch and time all the drops to see how long it takes them to evaporate. You can even try speeding them up with a blow drier!

Listen Carefully

Here is another old-fashioned saying that people once used to predict the weather! Break the Flip Flop code to learn what it is. Do you think this saying is true?

WHEN CLOUDS TRAVEL FAR AND WIDE, A STORMY DAY IT WILL BE OUTSIDE.

Words to Know

condensation

The physical change when water changes from a gaseous phase (invisible) to a liquid phase (drops of water). Dew is an example of condensation. Condensation is the opposite of evaporation.

DEW, FROST, AND FOG

In the Ping-Pong-ball-water molecule example, water went from a solid to a liquid to a gas. In each step, the Ping-Pong balls (water molecules) became more and more excited and moved faster. What if the opposite were to happen? What if excited and fast-moving water molecules started slowing down to a point where they put on yet another magic act? That's exactly what happens when water does the opposite of evaporate! When air is cooled and water molecules change from a gas to a liquid, it is called *condensation*. But how do you slow down those Ping-Pong balls, and what happens when they do slow down?

Imagine a nice warm summer evening with clear skies and dry conditions. Let's say you're camping out with your friends in your backyard under the open sky. Remember from Chapter 1 that there is always some water vapor making up part of the air around you. Imagine invisible Ping-Pong ball water molecules bouncing all over the place. As night comes and you fall asleep, the water molecules around you slow down as the temperature outside cools. All of those ball-like water molecules slow down to a point until they gather together, making little drops of liquid you can actually see. You wake up in the morning to drops of water all over the grass, your sleeping bag, and maybe even yourself! In other words, dew has formed! Dew is a perfect example of condensation, when water changes from a gas to a liquid.

Clouds and fog are two other important forms of condensation. They form as the air temperature cools down to a point where the invisible, fast-moving water molecules slow down and collect as little drops of water. Frost is just

Water Makes Weather

Choose from the letters W-A-T-E-R to fill in the blanks. Then look for the weather words hidden in each sentence. Hint: Each word in the list is hidden just one time.

HAIL FOG ICE MIST SNOW COLD RAIN
SLEET WIND CLOUD HUMID SUN THUNDER

__ow! In deep w__ter Kevin is now swimming!

I cer__ainly hop__ this box fits unde__ the bed.

Mimi s__opped to see __ cobr__ in Miami.

__he cats __ere bo__h unde__ the hous__.

T__o gruff og__es hum iden__ical __unes.

Be__h ails when she ea__s pe__nu__s or milk.

The te__che__ __as scolding Cedric loudly.

What a h__ssle! Ethan forget to pick me up!

Condensation Nuclei

Invisible dust, salt, and dirt particles in the air are called condensation nuclei. They are everywhere! In an air space the size of your finger, there are thousands of them! In every cloud and rain drop, a tiny, little speck of dirt exists! You are breathing in condensation nuclei right now!

Rising Air Cools

On most days, the temperature drops about 3–5°F for every 1,000 feet you go up. On a warm, sunny, 70°F day, it can be colder than the inside or your refrigerator just two miles above your head!

like dew, only the water turns to ice as it condenses out on cold objects like car windshields and metal surfaces that are below freezing. Next time you're scraping frost off of a car windshield, you'll know how it got there! It's all about water molecules and condensation.

Fog forms in much the same way as dew. Instead of the water molecules slowing down and gathering on sleeping bags, blades of grass, and car windows, they condense on tiny little microscopic dust and salt particles floating in the air. These little particles are known as *condensation nuclei* and they are everywhere in the air! When cooled air slows the Ping-Pong ball water molecules to a point where they gather on tiny dust particles in the air, presto, you've got fog. Fog is made up of billions and billions of tiny drops of water floating in the cooled air near the surface of the earth. Fog is yet another form of condensation and water's magic act!

THE MAKING OF CLOUDS

Have you ever been in a cloud? Have you ever swallowed some condensation nuclei? The answer to both of those questions is most likely a big YES! As you just learned, fog forms from invisible water in the air that condenses out as drops of liquid onto billions of tiny invisible dust particles. Clouds are simply a fog that forms in cool air high above the earth's surface. Each cloud is made up of billions and billions of tiny little droplets of water, each holding on to a tiny spec of dust in its center, floating through the atmosphere, carried along by the wind. Clouds are just like fog, only higher up in the sky! They are the result of condensation.

You already know that dew, frost, and fog usually form at night as the air cools down to allow condensation to occur, right? Why then can clouds form at any time of the day, not just on cool nights? Clouds can even form on warm sunny days with temperatures going up! How can you get air to cool down and condense, even on a warm, sunny day? How do clouds form? The answer is right above you! Look up, past your ceiling and roof and into the cold sky above.

When air is moved from the earth's surface up into the sky above, it often cools down. Even on a hot summer day, the temperature just a few miles above you is very chilly, even freezing! When air is lifted up into the sky, the molecules of water slow down and condense out into little drops of water and/or ice that we see as clouds. They can form at nearly any time of the day, take on many shapes and sizes, and even block out the sun and produce rain and snow. Clouds can form nearly anywhere, from just a few feet off the ground to over 10 miles up into the atmosphere over the earth! Clouds are amazing works of atmospheric condensation!

Have you ever really looked at and thought about the colors of clouds? Are all clouds white? You've probably seen clouds that are white, gray, purple, orange, and even pink. From up above the clouds, like in space, all clouds appear white. Clouds appear different colors because of the way sunlight hits the cloud. A bright white cloud may look dark gray or purple in parts simply because the sunlight can't get through it

Not Knot

Put each three-letter word into the grid next to its definition. Read the shaded column from top to bottom to get the silly answer to the riddle!

What bow can't be tied?

			Noah's boat
			Baseball hitter
			Quick swim
			Not the start
			Flow out
			Very low cloud
			Night bird

FOG   DIP   EBB

BAT   OWL

END

ARK

WHICH ONE ?

Which of the following U.S. cities has the cloudiest weather (almost 70 percent of the days are cloudy)?

1. Orlando, Florida
2. Astoria, Oregon
3. Scranton, Pennsylvania
4. St. Louis, Missouri

2. Astoria, Oregon

there. Rain clouds are so thick that sunlight can't pass through them, so the entire bottom of the cloud appears dark and gray, but they're white on top! What you're seeing is the shadow of the cloud on itself so it appears darker. When the sun is setting or rising it often makes clouds look pink or orange because of the long path sunlight must travel as it passes through the air. When you are above the clouds, like in an airplane or spaceship, most all clouds appear bright white, even storm clouds. They all look white from above because sunlight is reflected off of them into space, while the gray shadow ends up below the cloud on the earth's surface. Ah yes, the many shapes, sizes, and colors of clouds. Start looking up!

CLOUDS AND MORE CLOUDS

How many different types of clouds have you seen? Meteorologists have classified over two dozen different cloud types, but they can all fit into four main groups. The four main forms and types of clouds are cumulus, stratus, cirrus, and nimbus, and here are their key characteristics:

◆ **Cumulus clouds**—Look like cotton balls or chunks of cauliflower in the sky, often with grayish flat bottoms and puffy white tops. They form as warm air is lifted upward into the sky to cool and condense into drops of tiny water droplets. They usually form in sunny, dry weather.
◆ **Stratus clouds**—Layered out, flat-looking clouds that have a grayish color and are often spread out over the sky. They form from currents that move air across the

sky and not up and down like with a cumulus cloud. They often indicate that rain or snow may fall.

◆ **Cirrus clouds**—Thin, feathery, white clouds that usually form high in the sky. Because they form so far up in the atmosphere, they are usually made up of ice crystals and not droplets of water like most cumulus and stratus clouds. They often form a day or two before a storm system arrives.

◆ **Nimbus clouds**—Low, dark, grayish-looking clouds often called storm clouds. When you see these clouds, the air is usually condensed with moisture, and snow or rain is or will soon fall from the sky.

Cloud types are often combinations of the four main forms mentioned, for example cumulonimbus clouds.

Follow the Arrows

Use a light colored marker to connect the squares. Begin at the word START and follow the arrows. If a square has no arrow, keep going in the same direction until the next arrow. When you are done, read the words and word parts along the path to get the silly answer to the riddle.

What's the difference between a horse and the weather?

START

ONE	WISPY	CIRRUS	CLO
IS	REI	NED	UDS
ARE	NICK	UP	AND
NAM	ED	MARE'S	THE
DO	INS	TAILS	OTH
WN	RA	ONE	ER

Extra Fun: Read the leftover squares from left to right, and top to bottom.

Rain Clouds

Of all those clouds, only two types can make it rain, snow, sleet, and hail. They are nimbostratus and cumulonimbus. When these clouds form, the atmosphere has become filled or saturated with water from the process of condensation. Imagine you spilled some water on your kitchen table and started cleaning it up with a small towel. Once that towel has absorbed all the water it can, the rest will drip out and fall back on the table. In similar ways, once air is lifted and cooled into the sky above, it will form clouds. If the process continues, the clouds grow, thicken, and change form, becoming a nimbostratus or cumulonimbus cloud. In time, they let all that water out, just like a wet towel, and it will rain or snow, and maybe even cancel a picnic or two. Ah, the power of clouds.

CLOUD DIARY

Using the chart and information in this book, create a cloud diary. Each day in your diary, sketch and try to name the cloud type in the sky. Also, write down the type of weather that occurred with each type of cloud. You can then use your diary to help forecast the weather by the type of clouds that you see!

Clouds Taller Than a Mountain

Cumulonimbus clouds are the tallest clouds in the earth's atmosphere! While most clouds are only a few hundred or thousand feet thick, cumulonimbus clouds can grow to over 30,000 feet tall, or over 6 miles! That's taller than any mountain on the earth!

CHAPTER 4

Earth's Weather, from the Equator to the Poles

WHAT GOES UP MUST COME DOWN

You've heard it before: What goes up must come down! In meteorology and weather, that is true for many things, especially air. Do you remember what happens to air when it goes up? It often cools and condenses to form clouds and rain. The opposite occurs when air sinks downward; it usually warms up, dries out, and results in dry, clear conditions. Great rising and falling movements in the atmosphere help explain why wet, tropical rainforests can form right next to dry deserts like the Sahara in Africa. It's all about the ups and downs!

Have you ever watched how currents of air move near a campfire? Because the air over the center of the fire is the hottest, it rises upward into the sky, carrying smoke and particles along for the ride. That material rises up, spreads out, and then falls back toward the ground away from the center of the fire and heat. Meteorologists call these currents that move heat around *convection currents*. These currents move heat up and around near a campfire, but they also move heat up and down and all around our planet, creating different types of weather.

The earth's atmosphere is heated much like the air around a campfire. You already know that the earth gets its heat from the sun. The sun warms the earth's surface, and then that heat warms the air that is sitting on top of it, from the bottom up into the sky! And what part of the earth gets the most heat? You guessed it, the equator, the imaginary circle around the center of the earth. It's like the center of the campfire, getting more heat and making convection currents that move the air.

Try This

WATCHING CONVECTION

The next time an adult family member is cooking with boiling water, ask him or her to help you look into (but not touch) the pot of water. Watch the pasta or noodles moving around with the bubbles in the hot water. The currents of water moving everything around in the pot are convection currents. Up and down they go, just like the air currents in the atmosphere!

With more heat at the equator, and less heat elsewhere, you might be able to see how this can change the air around the earth. Like the air near the campfire, only in a much, much bigger way, the earth's atmosphere moves in large convection currents that move heat upwards into the sky from warm areas and downward and towards the surface in cooler areas. These large movements of air up and down across the earth form many different weather patterns, from deserts to rainforests. Are you in the ups or the downs, or somewhere in between?

World Weather

Use the decoder to figure out the words for WEATHER in Spanish, German, and French.

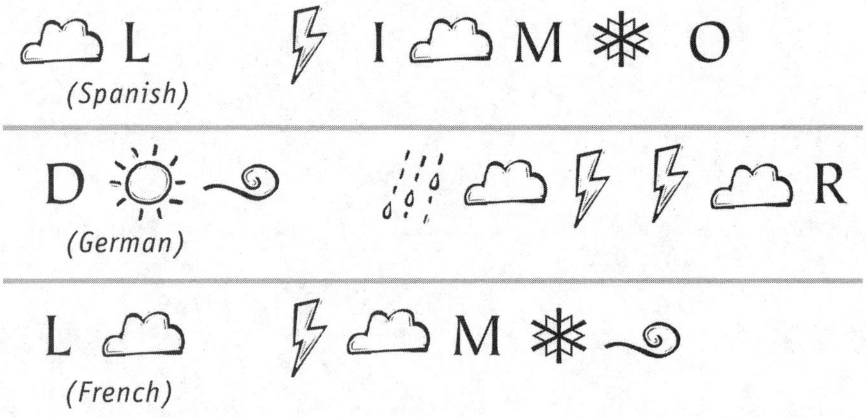

☁ L (Spanish) ⚡ I ☁ M ❄ O

D ☀ ～ ☔ ☁ ⚡ ⚡ ☁ R (German)

L ☁ ⚡ ☁ M ❄ ～ (French)

A ☀
E ☁
S ～
T ⚡
W ☔
P ❄

RAINFORESTS, DESERTS, AND EARTH'S WEATHER ZONES

Look at the following diagram, which shows the earth's main weather zones, and think of the campfire example discussed earlier and how air moves in convection currents. Also, you may want to go back to Chapter 2 and review what low- and high-pressure areas are and what the weather is like near them. It is very important in understanding how the earth's weather works.

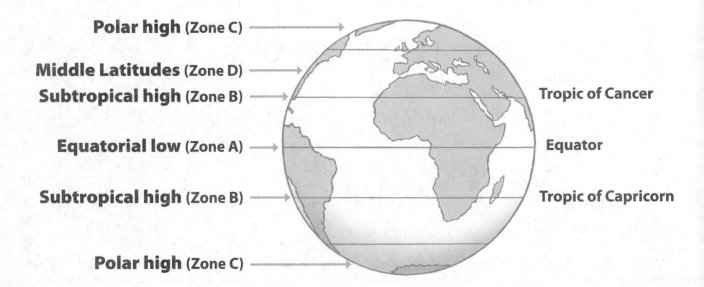

Polar high (Zone C)

Middle Latitudes (Zone D)

Subtropical high (Zone B) — Tropic of Cancer

Equatorial low (Zone A) — Equator

Subtropical high (Zone B) — Tropic of Capricorn

Polar high (Zone C)

◆ **Zone A. Equatorial Lows**—Because the equator of the earth is heated by the sun the most, its surface and atmosphere gets warmer than other areas around it. With all that heat gathering and rising upward (think campfire), it forms a band of low pressure, clouds, and rainfall that circle the earth near the equator like a tight-fitting belt. There, many of the world's tropical rainforests exist, and rainfall is often more that 100 inches per year! That's a lot of rainfall!

◆ **Zone B. Subtropical Highs**—Remember what happened to all that heat that went up near the center of the campfire? It stopped rising, spread out, cooled, and eventually came back down to the surface. In similar ways, much of the heated air that rises up near the equator spreads out, eventually cooling off and falling back toward the earth, forming areas of sinking air, high pressure, and dry weather. Many of these places form just north and south of the equator and are usually very dry and desert-like. Places like the Sahara Desert in Africa are very dry, with 1 inch of rain per year or less! There are some spots in this zone where it hasn't rained since you were born!

◆ **Zone C. Polar Highs**—Because the North and South Poles of the earth receive the least amount of heat from the sun, there is very little rising air or convection there compared with other areas. In this zone, the cold, sinking air often forms high pressure and dry, cold conditions.

◆ **Zone D. Middle Latitudes**—Much of the United States, Europe, and Asia are in this "in-between" weather zone. Cold air from the polar high zone often collides with the warmer air from the warmer subtropical highs forming a variety of weather that changes with the seasons. Warm and cold fronts, changing weather, and shifting seasons all play a part in this weather that will be discussed more later in this book.

Sahara Desert

The world's largest desert is the Sahara Desert in Africa. It is about the same size as the continental United States. Imagine a sea of sand across the United States from Los Angeles to Boston! The Sahara Desert lies in the horse latitudes, the high-pressure weather zone between 30° and 35° north and south of the equator where it is very dry!

WINDS ACROSS THE EARTH

Earlier in this book you learned that temperature and pressure differences cause the wind to blow. Could it be the same forces of nature that move clouds and storms right over your house or your town? Have you ever had a balloon slip out of your hands and drift into the sky? Which way did it go? Weather systems are carried along by winds much like that balloon. In which direction does your weather move? If a storm system is near your town, where will it go? Who gets it next? Which way will the wind currents take it?

In most of the United States, weather systems usually come in from the west and then drift away to the east. If it starts raining on a bird feeder in Pennsylvania in the morning, it'll usually be raining on the Statue of Liberty's torch in New York City later that afternoon. Weather usually moves west to east across much of the world, but wind patterns are very different and even opposite in many other parts of the world. Near the equator, storms move from the east to west! That's in the exact opposite direction of many other parts of the world, like the United States. Why would the winds reverse?

Think about how sailing ships traveled across the ocean back in Columbus's day. Traveling from Spain to the New World and then back again meant going in two different directions. Well, that's exactly how the winds blow across many parts of the earth. Near the equator, major winds blow from the east to west in a wind zone called the Easterlies. The Easterlies are also called the trade winds because early sailors used them to travel westward with their goods and valuables from the east. Storms and hurricanes often get car-

WHICH ONE?

Most storm systems move with the winds from west to east across the United States. About how fast do most storms actually move?

1. About as fast as a race car (100–200 miles per hour)
2. About as fast as a car moves through a small town (20–40 miles per hour)
3. About as fast as a person walking (2–5 miles per hour)
4. About as fast as a turtle walking (less than 1 mile per hour)

2. About as fast as a car moves through a small town (20–40 miles per hour)

ried along in the trade winds as they move from Africa to places like the United States, and in the opposite direction that most weather moves.

When some storms and hurricanes reach the United States from the east (being carried by the trade winds), they often change direction and get swept along by the west-to-east movement of wind. Why would they do this?

Just to the north and south of the trade winds, the winds travel in the opposite direction in a zone of west-to-east moving air called the Westerlies. Storms and weather systems get carried along across the United States in this west-to-east flow of air. Weather systems and storms in California often travel east across the United States and end up on the East Coast! A long journey of travel from west to east on the winds of the Westerlies. The following figure shows the pattern of the global winds.

F U N F A C T

Hurricanes and Columbus

Columbus had been warned by the indigenous people of the Carribean about "horrible tempests," translated into Spanish as "huracan," and Columbus experienced his first "huracan" on his fourth voyage. Columbus sought shelter and tried to warn the governor of Santo Domingo (on the island where the Dominican Republic and Haiti are located today) of the coming storm, but the governor turned Columbus away and even sent his own ships, full of gold (some belonging to Columbus), on to Spain. Of the thirty ships that sailed, the only ship that made it to Spain was the one that had Columbus's gold!

Global Winds

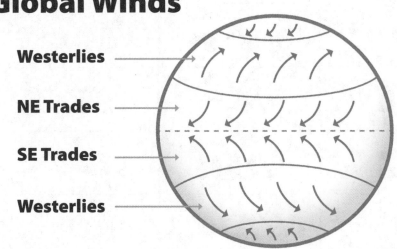

Westerlies

NE Trades

SE Trades

Westerlies

So True

Use the directions to cross words out of the grid. When you are done, read the remaining words from top to bottom, and left to right. You will learn a saying about the weather that is true all over the world!

Cross out...

...three-letter words that include the letter A

...words that start with WA

...words that rhyme with RAIN

WACKY	HAD	WHETHER	WAG
TEA	IT'S	SANE	COLD
OR	WHETHER	WANDER	TAN
FAN	LANE	IT'S	HOT
WE'LL	WALLPAPER	ALWAYS	TRAIN
WATER	HAVE	WASPISH	WEATHER
WHETHER	WE	OAR	LIKE
GAIN	IT	OR	MAIN
WASHER	HAT	WALL	NOT

BATTLE ZONES OVER THE UNITED STATES

Look again at the previous diagram showing how winds and pressure areas form across the earth and find your area on the map if you can. Now look below (south of) the United States near the areas of high pressure (subtropical highs). The weather there is usually dry and clear with sinking air and light winds. That's where many people go to vacation because of the warm temps, sunny skies, and little day-to-day change in the weather. Now you know why it's such a popular vacation area. Other parts of the world are not so calm and sunny most of the year!

Let's go back to the United States and much of Europe. Notice on the last diagram how the arrows of wind seem to collide near the northern parts of the United States and Canada. Colliding air results in active weather and storm systems with rain and snow. The cold polar Easterlies are trying their best to shove cold air form the north into the same area where the warmer air from the Westerlies and high pressure are. That's a battle zone! It's a push and shove match that has been going on forever, and it produces much of the changing weather across the United States and Europe!

It is that very battle zone area that produces much of the day-to-day changes in weather across much of the United States, especially across the northern states. During the autumn and winter months, the polar Easterlies often push farther south, bringing cold air and snow from the north. Once the spring and summer months arrive, the Westerlies and high-pressure areas shift more northward, pushing the cold air and active weather back into Canada and places north.

Try This

VACATION WEATHER

Think of as many places that you can where many people go on vacation to enjoy warm, sunny, dry weather. Next, try and find the vacation spots on a map of the world. You should find out that many of the spots you named are between the United States and the equator in the weather zone known as the *horse latitudes*. Remember, high pressure and dry weather exist there.

Smooth and Flat

When the trade winds from the south reach the equator, they bump into the trade winds from the north. This makes air move steadily upward, not flat along the surface. This area of unusually calm and non-windy weather can cause a lot of frustration for the powerful sailboats in round-the-world races! Break the Smooth and Flat code to learn the name for this special weather system.

JET STREAM DIPS AND DIVES

You've heard it many times in weather forecasts. You've probably even seen it winding like a snake of arrows on weather maps. It may even be over your house right now! What is this popular, ever-changing, weather maker? It's the jet stream! The jet stream is an important part of the earth's weather, moving many weather systems and storms along as it flows like a river of air above your head! There are a few different types of jet streams, but the main ones form near that "battle zone" you've just read about in the last section. The jet stream forms in the strong temperature differences near the colliding polar Easterlies and warmer Westerlies. The stronger the temperature differences, the faster and more energetic the jet stream and its wind grows!

Like a ribbon wrapped around a present, jet streams often wrap around the entire earth, forming a wavy pattern over 20,000 miles long. Yes, that's long enough to wrap around and join many of the countries you've learned about in school! The winds flowing through the jet stream can move at over 150 miles per hour. That's three times faster than most cars traveling on a highway! You never directly feel jet stream winds because they flow a couple of miles or more above your head, but they can move weather systems and storms along like a leaf caught in a fast flowing river.

Since the main jet streams are really part of the Westerlies, they flow in a west-to-east pattern across many of the middle-latitude parts of the earth, including the United States, Europe, and Asia. The winds of the jet stream usually bend upward and downward into a winding pattern called ridges and troughs. A *ridge* forms when the jet stream bends upward in a loop towards the poles. Usually, warm and dry

FUN FACT
The Jet Stream
The jet stream was discovered by accident by World War II jet pilots. As they traveled from east to west toward Japan, they were slowed down by strong winds at 30,000 feet (6 miles). They were actually flying into the winds we now know as the jet stream.

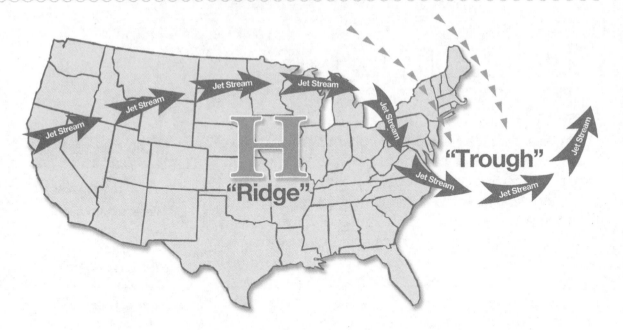

weather forms near a ridge. When the jet stream makes a dip or dive, it's called a *trough*. These troughs often bring colder temperatures, strong fronts, and storms systems that can produce rain and snow!

Trough Weather

The word *trough* can be used to describe the jet stream as well as large bowls that farm animals and horses eat and drink out of. When the jet stream forms a trough, it looks much like a feeding container, as the winds flow in the shape of the sides and bottom of the bowl. In a jet stream trough, instead of food, there's a bowl of cold air bending down from the north. Troughs can be as large and deep as the entire United States and create a large area of unique weather. On the east or right side of the trough (bowl), rain, snow, and storms often form and move along with the jet stream winds. In the bowl of the trough, it's often cold and cloudy. Watch for them in your local weather reports and remember, it's all about the trough!

Opposite Weather

The size of one jet stream trough and one ridge together is often about the same size as the United States. Because of this, completely opposite weather patterns often form. If a trough forms in the western part of the United States, it's often cloudy and rainy, while the eastern parts enjoy warm, sunny weather with the ridge. It's often a perfect opposite!

58

CHAPTER 5

You Can't Get Away from Them: Fronts

WHY FRONTS ARE IMPORTANT

Can you remember a day when the weather started out warm and sunny but ended up with rain, wind, and cooler temperatures? What happened? How can weather change so quickly? Chances are that a front moved through. In some areas, a different front will sweep through with changing weather every week or so. But what is a front? Where do fronts come from, and how do fronts change your weather and affect your life?

Imagine a tied-up garbage bag filled with stinky broccoli that went bad. Inside that bag is a bubble of air with certain characteristics, like stinky broccoli odors. If you opened the bag up, the smelly air would move out of the bag and into its surroundings, including your nose. It just invaded your space! You were hit with a broccoli front! It came in and changed the air from one characteristic to another. That's what fronts do!

The same sort of thing happens in the earth's atmosphere that happens to smelly broccoli. Instead of a bag of smelly broccoli, it's a huge chunk of air called an air mass with special characteristics. Air masses are very large, usually hundreds of miles across, and contain air that is different from the air they're moving into. Some are cold and dry, others are warm and moist, but when they push their way into another type of air mass, a front forms. The leading edge of an air mass is called a *front*. It could be a warm front, cold front, or even a broccoli front, but when it moves in, you'll notice the difference! There are four main types of fronts, each with its own type of weather pushing its way into your town, your picnic, and your school.

The Word *Front*

Before the word *front* was used in weather, it had been used as a term in warfare. During World War I and II, the term *front* was used to describe a line of soldiers advancing into foreign territory. Weather fronts advance into foreign territory too, but with large chunks of air!

THE COLD FRONT

By its name, you've probably already figured out what it is, right? Yes, a cold front is the leading edge of a colder air mass that is pushing its way into a different type of air mass. But what does a cold front do to your weather? What does it look like on a weather map? How could it be used to forecast the weather? Many cold fronts have passed over your town since you've been there, and many more will be coming in the future. Let's see how they work!

Have you ever opened up the freezer door on your refrigerator and felt the cold air drain down onto your toes? Cold air is heavy and dense, and it likes to stay low and near the ground. When a cold air mass is pushed along by the jet stream or winds in the atmosphere, its front edge is called a *cold front*, which moves forward, pushing all of the other air in its path away. In the same way that a snowplow pushes snow up and around the plow blade, the air in front of a cold front

MAKE YOUR OWN COLD AIR MASS

With your parents help, put a few drops of food coloring into a small glass of water. Place that glass of water in your refrigerator for at least an hour or so. Now, very slowly pour the water that was in your refrigerator (with food coloring in it) down the sides of another glass filled with warm water. Watch as the colder, colored water drains down into the bottom of the warmer water. You've just make an advancing mass of cold water, or a water cold front!

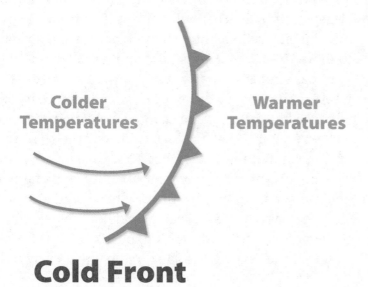

Colder Temperatures   **Warmer Temperatures**

Cold Front

is forced up, cooling it and condensing it into a band of rain or snow (depending on the season). That's why cold fronts produce precipitation. Remember, a cold front is a cooler air mass on the move, pushing all of the air ahead of it and around it up and out of the way as it moves in!

On a weather map, cold fronts are often shown as long blue lines with little blue triangles on them. They usually move to the east, traveling nearly 300–500 miles in about one day. Remember, these fronts usually bring a brief band of rain or snow, followed by temperatures that are colder than they were before the front moved through. Look around for a weather map today and see if you can find cold fronts and use them to predict your weather.

THE WARM FRONT

As you've learned in the previous section, cold air behind a cold front is heavier than warm air, pushing it aside as it sweeps through. What will happen if warm air starts moving and pushing its way into heavy colder air that doesn't want to move? Yes, warm air is light and doesn't "hug" the ground like cold air does. When a warm air mass moves, it forms weather that is very different from that of a cold front. The advance of a warm air mass into a colder air mass is called a *warm front*. It's that battleground near the front that makes exciting and different weather.

Think about what happens when water along the beach crashes against a pile of sand or a newly made sandcastle. The mounds of sand are heavy and hold their ground while the water (not as heavy) tries to push into it. Over time, the water will ramp over the sand and break it away to nothing!

Try This

DRAWING FRONTS

Get out some crayons, markers, and pencils and start drawing some make-believe fronts! You can draw and color fronts like they really appear on a weather map, or make up your own symbols using rectangles, squares, triangles, and other shapes. You can even ask your parents for old newspapers with weather maps on them and color them, too!

Think of warmer air as the water and colder air as the sand in the earth's atmosphere. When a chunk of warmer air (like water) moves into colder air (sand castle), it glides up and over it, like a large ramp, and over time pushes all of the cold air aside and wears it away like the sand in the sand castle! With all of the warmer air going up and over the colder air, it cools and forms clouds and precipitation. That's why warm fronts bring rain or snow also, just like cold fronts.

On weather maps, warm fronts are usually shown as long red lines with little half circles on them. Remember, that line is the leading edge of warmer air that is pushing into colder air (waves of water into sand mounds). Warm fronts usually move slower than cold fronts and bring longer periods of rain and snow as they move to the east and northeast. Look for warm fronts on weather maps and use this book to help predict your weather as they pass by your house!

Colder Air

Warm Front

Warmer Air

OCCLUDED AND STATIONARY FRONTS

Occluded? Sure it's a big funny word, but now that you understand both the cold and warm fronts, you can easily understand what an occluded front is! Do you remember which type of front moves the fastest? You got it, a cold front! When a cold front catches up to a warm front, they are said to *occlude*. That means the cold air has pushed all of the warm air aside and is sort of running out of gas. In a way, the air masses with both fronts sort of join and mix together as one as the fronts start to die out!

The following diagram shows how an occluded front looks on a weather map. Note that the line showing the front is really a combination of a cold and warm front symbols, having both triangles and half circles. The weather near an

Which Way Did It Go?

On a weather map, the symbols drawn on the front usually point in the direction that the front is moving. Cold fronts often are shown with pointed blue triangles that point in the direction of movement.

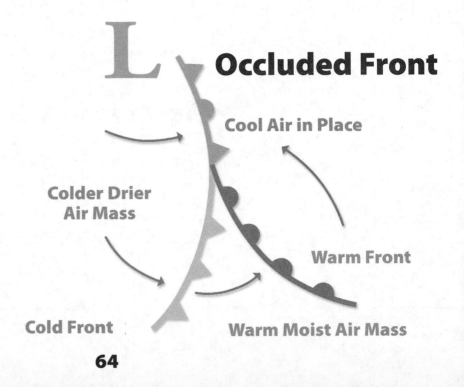

L **Occluded Front**

Cool Air in Place

Colder Drier Air Mass

Warm Front

Cold Front

Warm Moist Air Mass

occluded front is often a combination of warm front and cold front weather, with both ramped-up clouds and showers of rain and snow.

So, occluded fronts form from fronts moving at different speeds. But what if a front doesn't move at all? Stop reading and moving for a few seconds! You are said to be stationary, or not moving. Start moving and reading again. When air masses are face to face, but not moving, a stationary front forms between them. With *stationary fronts*, clouds and showers form, but there is often no real change in weather since the air masses are not moving much. The symbol for a stationary front is similar to an occluded front, but the triangles and half circles are on opposite sides of the line showing the front. Look for them on some weather maps and see how they don't move much over a few days.

WHICH ONE ?

Which type of front usually forms in Canada and moves south into the United States?

1. Cold front
2. Warm front
3. Occluded front
4. Stationary front

1. Cold front

Slow Down!

Towering thunderheads, powerful storms, gale force winds—the forces that are generated when a front is on the move are awesome! Can anything slow down this wild weather? Turns out that two things can! Use a bright colored marker to highlight all the letters that are not C, G, or H. Read the colored letters from top to bottom and left to right.

```
M C O G H U H G N
G T H A C H I C H
N H G H S H C G H
G W G C H A R H C
H C M G B H O C D
I H E H C S C O G
C G C F G H W G C
G A C T C E C H R
```

THE PERFECT STORM

Spin Cycles

Storm systems have wind and air that spin counterclockwise in the Northern Hemisphere and clockwise in the Southern Hemisphere. Near the equator, storm systems usually don't spin at all!

When most people use the word *storm*, they're talking about a low-pressure area, or a "low." And when you see a low pressure or *L* on a weather map, it is hardly ever alone! Most lows have fronts sticking out of them. Yes, the same fronts you just learned about: warm, cold, occluded, and stationary. Let's see how they make up the "perfect storm."

In the Northern Hemisphere, low-pressure areas have winds around them that spin counterclockwise, or in the opposite direction that the hands on a clock move (see Chapter 2). Imagine the spinning arms of a large windmill or

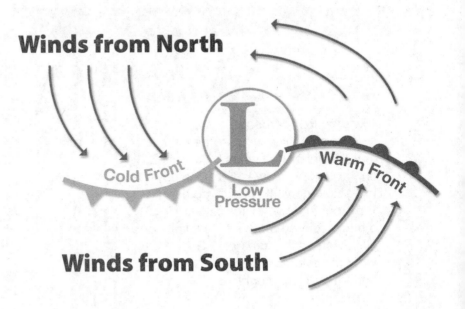

Winds from North

Cold Front

L

Low Pressure

Warm Front

Winds from South

water spinning around in a flushed toilet. In a low-pressure area, the air spins in similar ways. Look at the following diagram and picture in your mind all of those arrows moving air around the center of low pressure. On the left side of the low, air is moving from north to south, while on the right side, air is moving from south to north. As that air moves and swirls around the low, it collides with the air around it, forming many of the fronts you just learned about.

When you see this type of storm system, you will notice that hanging down like a tail from the low is a cold front. That's where the colder air is circulating winds from north to south. On the right side of the low, warm air is circulating up from the south, making a warm front stick out of the right from the center of the low. Putting this all together, you end up with a "perfect looking" storm system that has all types of weather wrapped around it as it spins counterclockwise and moves across most places like the United States, Europe, and Asia.

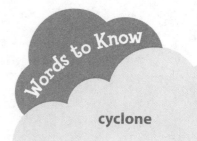

Words to Know

cyclone

A cyclone is the name given to many different types of storms. All cyclones are areas of low pressure with bands of clouds, rain, and air spinning and swirling around their center. Hurricanes, typhoons, and low-pressure areas can all be called cyclones.

YOU TILTED WHAT?

There's one thing that changes the overall weather pattern of fronts, low-pressure areas, and jet streams more than nearly anything else! It can lower temperatures by over a hundred degrees and change a mountain of snow and cold into a peaceful retreat of flowers and chirping birds! It can melt glaciers the size of states and cause life on the earth to change its entire behavior or even move to a whole new location. This weather force can even make you change your entire wardrobe, lifestyle, and how you live from day to day! Is it a cold front? Is it a high-pressure system? Is it a new jet stream current? Oh, it's much bigger a force than those examples! It's the earth's tilt! Yes, your planet is leaning on its side!

The planet you are on right now seems to have been knocked on its side millions and millions of years ago! Oh, it didn't tip over, but it is leaning a bit as it spins on its axis of rotation. To understand the earth's tilt, think of a basketball with a black dot placed on opposite ends, at the exact top and bottom of the ball. Now imagine the ball spinning around quickly with one black dot at the bottom touching the ground and the other end straight up on top! If it helps,

On Either Side

When two different masses of air meet on either side of a front, they often create a storm. What determines how strong this storm is? Read the numbered words in order to find out!

13. the   3. the   4. difference   6. the

14. storm!   11. more   8. and   2. greater

5. between   9. humidity,

7. temperature   1. The   10. the   12. powerful

picture a large nail sticking into the ball from the top dot through the bottom dot and the basketball spinning and spinning around that nail, the axis of rotation. As it looks now, the nail is perfectly straight up and down into the ball as it spins around and around!

What if you grabbed that nail and tilted it and the ball so that it leans a bit on its side as it rotates? That is what the earth is doing! The earth's tilt of rotation is about 23½ degrees. For the basketball, that's like tilting the nail going into the top black dot about 6 inches or so from the top, making it lean to its side as it rotates. That's a big lean-over! Because the earth leans a bit to its side as it rotates, different parts of the planet receive different amounts of light from the sun. During nearly half of the year, one hemisphere (top or bottom) leans toward the sun while the other half leans away from the sun. When the Northern Hemisphere (United States, Europe, Asia) of the earth leans toward the sun, more direct and longer-lasting light causes a warming pattern and the summer months occur! As the earth revolves around the sun, six months later, everything reverses and the Northern Hemisphere ends up tilting away from the sun, thus receiving less light and warmth and bringing on the winter months! Yes, it's the tilted nail in the basketball causing everything!

Because of the earth's tilt, and the resulting changing seasons, the weather patterns across the earth are constantly changing! For example, when winter arrives in the United States, the earth's Northern Hemisphere tilts away from the sun, daylight shortens, the sun gets weaker in the sky, and cold air masses build and move south. The jet stream moves south, too, forming big bends (ridges and troughs) that allow storm systems and fronts to form and move across the United States. Snowstorms, strong winds,

Try This

BASKETBALL EARTH

Ask your parents if you can draw a little dot at the top and bottom of a basketball (or any larger ball). Now, try and spin the ball with a perfect zero-tilt rotation, keeping the dot at the exact top of the ball as it rotates. Now tilt the ball and spin it with the dot tilted a bit to the side, just like the earth's tilt of rotation. Throughout the earth's history, it has had many different tilts of rotation, just like the ball!

What Is a Derecho?

A derecho (pronounced day-RAY-cho) is a widespread windstorm caused by a fast-moving band of severe thunderstorms. These storms are huge—their paths are at least 280 miles long, and from 50–300 miles wide! Here is an important fact: derechos are characterized by damaging straight-line winds. Why is this important to know? Break the Number Substitution code (1=A, 2=B, etc.) to find out!

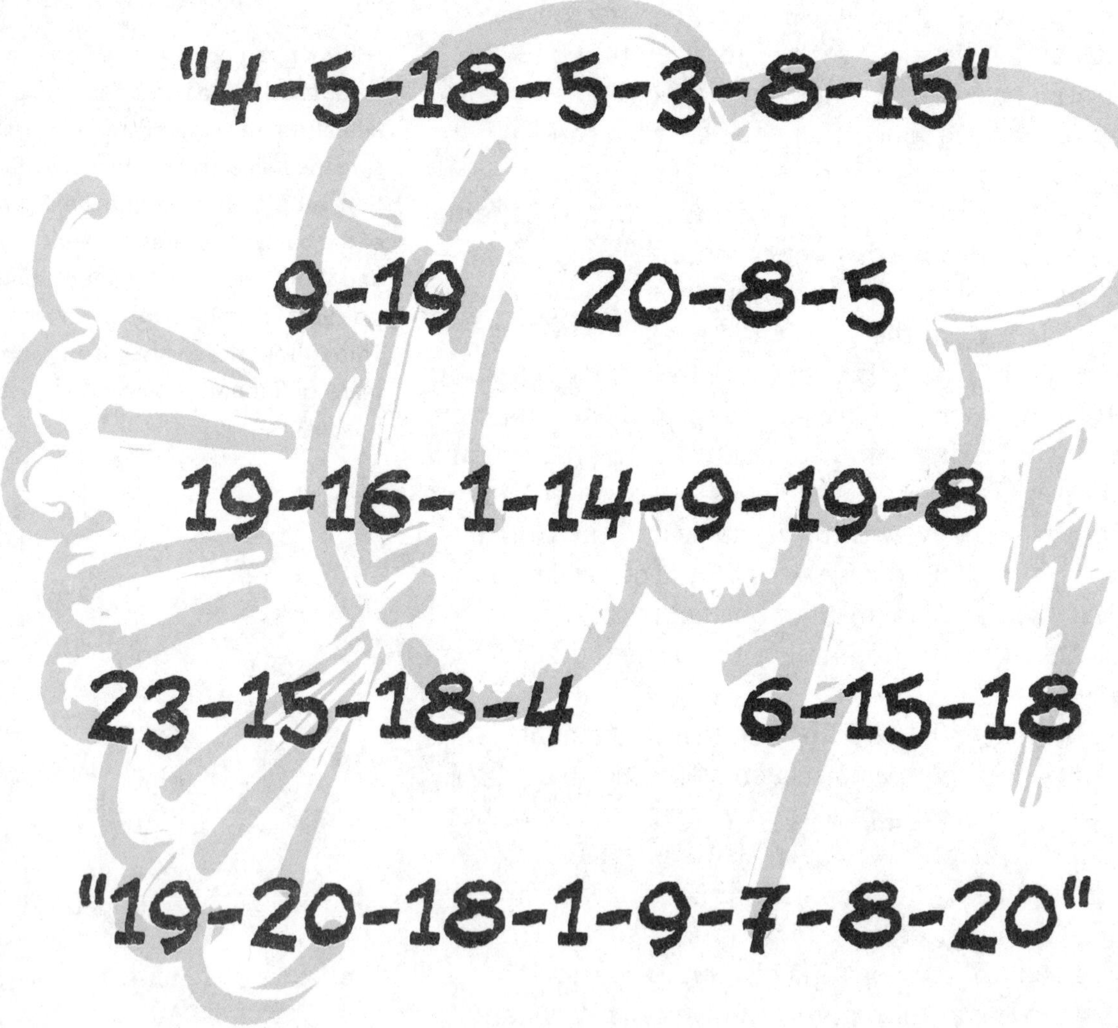

"4-5-18-5-3-8-15"

9-19   20-8-5

19-16-1-14-9-19-8

23-15-18-4   6-15-18

"19-20-18-1-9-7-8-20"

energetic cold fronts, and frigid temperatures all help to slow life and action down during the winter months. During the summer months everything reverses. Daylight and sun strength increases as the Northern Hemisphere tilts toward the sun. The jet stream moves north, allowing the weather patterns to calm down and temperatures to rise! Although thunderstorms and severe weather can increase with the warmer summer conditions, most living things, including meteorologists, have more time to relax and enjoy longer daylight and less active weather. Just think: it's all because of a nail-like tilt placed 23½ degrees in a rotating basketball earth!

FUN FACT

Biggest Tilt in the Solar System

The planet Uranus has a tilt of rotation nearly four times greater than that of Earth! Uranus is tilted on its side as it orbits the sun, as if it were laying down while rotating on its axis! Because of this unusual tilt, one hemisphere of Uranus is in darkness for many years while the other side stays in light!

CHAPTER 6

Weather Maps and Forecasting: Do It Yourself

HOW A METEOROLOGIST PREDICTS THE WEATHER

Try This

MAKE A FOOD FORECAST

Early in the morning, start your day by making a breakfast, lunch, and dinner food forecast. Without asking your parents or family members, try and predict what you'll be eating for the rest of the day. You'll have to gather information from what's in your refrigerator, pantry, on schedules, and what has happened in the past! See how accurate your forecast came out to be later in the day!

What is a prediction? Have you ever made a prediction? Pretend it's Saturday morning and you have to make a prediction about what you are going to eat for the rest of the day. What are you going to have for breakfast? What are you having for lunch? What about dinner? Are you going out to eat for one of those meals? How would you start making predictions and forecasts?

Before you can predict what you'll be eating for the day, you'll need to collect some information. You'd probably start by talking to your family members. You would also check your schedules, see what's in the refrigerator, and maybe even look at what's in the oven. Once you've gathered all of the information you could, you can then make a prediction about what you're going to eat throughout that Saturday. You can then make a food forecast!

If there's no milk in the refrigerator early in the morning, you could predict that you will probably not be having cereal for breakfast! That is a prediction or forecast that is based on information, facts, and some past experience. Before meteorologists can make a forecast about what the weather will do for the day, they must first gather facts and information about the weather, just like checking the refrigerator for milk was important in making a food forecast. Meteorologists collect information about things like air pressure, winds, jet stream currents, clouds, moisture patterns, fronts, and high-

and low-pressure areas! Do these things sound familiar? These are all of the weather elements you've been reading and learning about in this book! They are all needed to make a weather forecast!

Now pretend that there is a strong low-pressure area (remember, stormy conditions) on the West Coast of the United States, near California. Where will it move? How fast will it travel? Will the jet stream winds carry it away from the rest of the United States, or will the fronts near the low reach Denver, Colorado, and produce rain and snow? Is the air temperature so cold that snow and ice will form? These are all good questions that a meteorologist must ask before making a weather forecast. But first you need information.

WEATHER STATIONS AND OBSERVATIONS

How can you get information to make a food forecast? Parents, brothers, sisters, schedules, and observing all can give you some information about what you'll be eating for the day. Meteorologists get their information from many different places, too. Listed below are some of the important types of information meteorologists use to start making a weather forecast.

MAKE YOUR OWN WEATHER OBSERVATIONS

Make a daily weather observation. At the same time each day, go outside and write down in a notebook the current weather conditions. You can record things like sky cover, cloud type, temperature, winds, barometer reading, and more! Some of the readings you can even get from your local weather stations. Watch how they change from day to day!

♦ **Observations.** All over the earth's surface are weather observation stations. Many are at airports and schools. Others are at parks and in towns. Some are even on the ocean, floating on a buoy. Observation stations record what is happening outside with the weather. Things like temperature, air pressure, wind, moisture,

Weather Satellites

The first successful weather satellite was called TIROS-1 and was launched into orbit around Earth in 1960. Today there are thousands of satellites looking down on Earth. Look up into the sky and imagine a few of them looking down onto your weather right now!

and rainfall are all measured by meteorologists or are automatically recorded by computers! These observations are very important in gathering weather information that is used in making a weather forecast.

◆ **Weather satellites.** Imagine being thousands of miles up in space and looking down onto Earth to watch weather patterns as they form and move from place to place! Weather satellites do just that. Many are circling Earth and might be right above you as you read this book! Weather satellites are small spaceships with special cameras placed in orbit around Earth that watch and monitor the weather below. Satellites help meteorologists to study weather systems from above the clouds.

◆ **Radar.** Radar is a word that stands for RAdio Detection And Ranging. It's not as confusing as it sounds. Have you ever yelled into a canyon or large room and heard your voice echo back at you? In the same way, meteorologists can "yell" or transmit invisible radio waves at a storm system using radar. When those radio waves hit tiny drops of rain and snow in storm systems, they "echo" back to the radar unit. Using the echo of radar, meteorologists can make a map of where the rain and snow is and how fast it's moving!

It's Simple

Barometers, satellite information, radar, and gauges to measure wind speed and rainfall are some of the tools a meteorologist will use to tell about the weather. But you can learn about the weather in your neighborhood by using a simple piece of rope. How? Figure out where the puzzle pieces go and write the letters in the empty grid!

How can you use a rope to tell the weather?

WEATHER MAPS: WHAT YOU SEE IS WHAT YOU GET

Using weather observations, satellite images, and radar maps, meteorologists start putting together weather maps. You've seen weather maps in books, on television, in the newspaper, and on computers. In many ways, a weather map is like a treasure map, showing the map reader where interesting things are located. Instead of treasures full of gold, weather maps show air pressure, fronts, temperatures, winds, jet streams, and all of the information meteorologists need. An example of a typical weather map used by a meteorologist is shown below. Let's work with it!

Like on the following map, just about every weather map will have a few Hs and Ls on it. Remember, they stand for

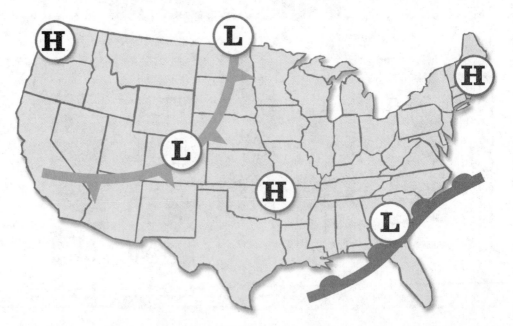

areas of high and low pressure. The Ls or low-pressure areas will often have cold and warm fronts, clouds, and stormy weather nearby. The Hs will often be surrounded by clear, dry weather and high pressure. Often temperatures, precipitation areas, wind conditions, clouds, and moisture are displayed on weather maps, too. A meteorologist can look at a weather map and quickly find out how the atmosphere is behaving, where weather systems are, and see how conditions are changing. Storms, sunny skies, cold temperatures, clouds, and rain patterns are like treasures on a weather map if you know how to read it.

On a treasure map and a weather map, what you see is what you get, but what about what you're *going* to get? How will the things on the map change in a day or two. Imagine a treasure map with an X marking the spot of a treasure. Now, each day the treasure is moved to a new location. In a way, that's how weather maps change from day to day. A low-pressure system with rain in Texas may move to the east and produce stormy weather to a new area in a day or two. A cold front in Canada can move into the United States and bring cold weather all the way from the Great Lakes to Florida as it travels south! Yes, the treasures move! Meteorologists study the weather pattern and weather maps and forecast the weather.

Meteorologists learn in school and in their training how to read weather maps and follow weather patterns. With all of their knowledge, observations, and special computers, meteorologists decide how things on a weather map will be changing and who's getting the next treasure! The treasure might be a high-pressure system with sunshine, or it might be a cold front with snow and frigid temperatures. Like a treasure map, weather maps contain a lot of information. Understanding the maps and everything on them is very important in forecasting the weather!

WHICH ONE?

If you see a cold front passing over your town on a weather map, what will your forecast include?

1. Rainy, warm weather
2. Cloudy, then warmer weather
3. Sunny, cold weather
4. Rainy, then colder weather

4. Rainy, then colder weather

JET STREAM MAPS: WHAT YOU DON'T SEE IS WHAT YOU GET

Picture yourself standing near a stream or river looking down into the water. Now imagine all of the pebbles and rocks you see in the water at the bottom of the stream bed as towns and buildings. In many ways, the atmosphere moves just like the water in a stream. The water flows around the rocks and stream bed, carrying items along in the water. Maybe a large leaf will float by. Maybe a log will spin through after that!

Jet Stream

In the atmosphere, storms, cyclones, and fronts are like the leaves and logs, drifting by on currents in the air. The air and atmosphere high above the ground moves weather along on river-like currents of air known as the jet stream. To forecast the weather, meteorologists must know where these currents are, how fast they are moving, and how they will change.

You can't really see the jet stream flowing above you, but you can watch it carry things along with it. Remember, the sky above your head is flowing like the water in a stream or river sweeping storms, clouds, and everything in the sky along with it! Have you ever wondered what happened to that helium party balloon that you let go outside when you were younger? Yes, it drifted up into the sky and was carried along by the jet stream. Twice a day, meteorologists all over

Rain, Rain, Go Away

There are different kinds of rain showers, from gentle drizzles to steady downpours. People always want to know when the rain will stop so they can go back outside. Here's an old-time weather saying that gives you a hint how long a certain kind of storm will last. To read it, break the Shift-One-Letter code.

B TVO TIJOZ TIPXFS

XPO'U MBTU

IBMG BO IPVS.

Words to Know

contrail

Look up into the sky and watch for the moisture that forms a long, thin, ribbon-like cloud from the exhaust of a jet airplane. Many people think it is smoke, but it is really mainly a stream of water vapor called a contrail. Contrails often form at the same height as the jet stream and usually move it!

the world release weather balloons that drift upward into the sky. By tracking the balloons and the weather instruments on them, they can find how and where the jet stream currents are moving and flowing. Maps showing the position and movement of the jet stream are then made and used in making weather forecasts. Following is an example of a weather map showing the jet stream currents.

The previous jet stream map shows a storm system (low-pressure area) near Texas. Where will it go? If you were a meteorologist making a forecast, what would you predict? Remember, storms and weather systems move along with the "invisible" jet stream like leaves in a river, or like cars following a road. When you look down a road or highway, it usually has many curves and turns in it. The jet stream often flows with curves and turns similar to a winding road. Weather systems that form near the jet stream follow the road of air as it turns and curves across the earth. That storm system near Texas would move along with the jet stream north and east into the state of Missouri. Did you forecast that? Congratulations, you're using the jet stream to make weather forecasts!

The jet stream is always changing its shape and form. Like a snake slithering across the ground, the jet stream moves and bends in different ways from day to day. Meteorologists not only have to forecast storms and weather systems that move with the jet stream, but they have to forecast how the jet stream will change its shape from day to day. Think about it, all that jet stream action up above your head and you can't even see it. As you read this sentence, it's moving storms, clouds, and weather along, bending like a snake and carrying mountains of air thousands of miles! Go ahead, look out your window and picture that invisible river of air above!

Hink Pinks

A Hink Pink is a funny kind of riddle—the answer is always two single-syllable words that rhyme! Choose your answers from the words scatterd around the page. We did the first one for you.

DRAIN   SNOW   CLOUD   STORM

FOG   NEAT

1. Hole down which storm water flows

RAIN   DRAIN
_____   _____

2. White flakes that don't fall fast

_____   _____

3. Icy rain that falls in a tidy manner

ICE

_____   _____

4. Tropical weather event

LOUD

_____   _____

WARM

5. Water vapor in the sky that makes thunder

_____   _____

NICE

6. Friendly frozen water

BOG

_____   _____

7. Water vapor lying low over a swamp

SLOW

_____   _____

THE MAGIC OF THE GREEN SCREEN

Think about this for a few moments. Where have you seen most weather forecasts? What about weather maps with long arrows showing where and how the jet stream is flowing? You've probably seen large blobs of green and yellow on radar maps showing rain heading toward your town. There's even a place that shows nothing but weather maps and forecasts all day long. Where? You've probably seen it all on your television! And who's showing you all of that weather information? There's usually a weather person or meteorologist standing in front of all of those weather maps on television. How do they do that?

Most weather forecasters that you see on television are standing in front of a large flat wall that is painted blue or green. It's often called a green screen. Right in front of the weather forecaster is a television camera pointed toward him or her and the blue or green screen. What the camera sees is what you see at home on your television. But you don't see blue or green, do you? A special computer hooked up to the camera takes away the green or blue color and puts weather maps in its place, but only to someone watching on television. When you watch the weather forecaster on television, it looks like there are weather maps behind him, even though in reality the weather forecaster is standing in front of just a blue or green wall!

How does the weather forecaster know where to point near a green screen? How does he or she see the weather maps that you see on your television to explain the weather forecast? Usually there is a monitor off to the side of the green screen, out of view of the camera. The meteorologist

FUN FACT

Blue Screens in the Movies

Have you ever seen a movie showing people right next to dinosaurs, monsters, or make-believe scenes? Most of the time they are actors standing in front of a large green or blue screen, just like television weather forecasters. In place of weather maps, computer-made monsters and scenes are added to the green screen later on!

or weather forecaster stands in front of and points on the green screen while looking off to the side at the monitor at the weather map you see on the television. It takes a while to get used to and a lot of coordination, but all you see is the weather forecaster standing in front of storms, high-pressure systems, and all types of weather maps. Now you know the TV meteorologist's secret.

Next time you watch a weather forecaster on television, try and notice some things. Notice how the areas of high and low pressure (Hs and Ls) result in different types of weather. Notice how the forecaster shows weather systems moving along with the jet stream. Locate and think about what type of fronts are on the map and where they are going. Also, imagine a green screen behind the forecaster. Watch how he or she will be looking off to the side of the maps, but not really at the maps, as they watch themselves on television. It's all a part of a weather forecast—the weather maps, storms, jet streams, the clouds, the bands of rain and snow, and the magic of the green screen!

CHAPTER 7

Severe Weather

THE INGREDIENTS OF SEVERE WEATHER

What is severe weather? If something is *severe*, it usually goes beyond what normally happens. It also usually means some sort of action is needed to handle the severe activity. In our atmosphere, severe conditions often happen with special types of weather systems. Can you think of these special types of storms? These are storms that make you take action! Storms that make you gather supplies, protect yourself, or even leave your home for a safer place. The four main types of weather systems that cause severe weather are hurricanes, tornadoes, thunderstorms, and snowstorms! Let's learn about severe weather and how it happens!

Since most of the time severe weather does NOT occur, something special must happen to make the weather turn really active and severe. Can you think a few things that happen to the atmosphere to make it get "sparked up" and turn into severe weather? What ingredients go into making special weather events? Think about what hurricanes, tornadoes, thunderstorms, and even snowstorms all have in common. Time's up! Most can produce strong winds. Others can let out great amounts of rain. Some are associated with low pressure and rising air. One thing they all can do is produce great amounts of damage and loss to human property and objects in their path.

Just like an automobile needs fuel and air to make it run, the atmosphere needs some special ingredients to run really active and make severe weather. Many of the topics you read about in this book can lead to these special ingredients. The jet stream often needs to be flowing just right. The humidity

WHICH ONE ?

Which of the following weather conditions is most likely to produce severe weather?

1. High-pressure area
2. Jet stream ridge
3. Strong cold front
4. Fast-moving cirrus clouds

3. Strong cold front

and moisture in the air needs to be pumped up high! The air pressure needs to be low, allowing air to rise up into the sky and cool and condense out into large clouds. Also, temperature and location are very important in making severe weather. When all of the conditions are just right, the sky can grow angry and lead to the formation of weather events that can bring down buildings, flood towns, and close highways and schools!

Although hurricanes, tornadoes, thunderstorms, and snowstorms are all very different from each other, they all have similar characteristics and have caused their share of damage on this planet over the years. While hurricanes can be as large as the state of Texas and cause widespread flooding and wind damage, tornadoes are often as small as buildings but can tear a barn to shreds! Thunderstorms can heat up a maple tree to over a thousand degrees with a flash of lightning, while snowstorms can cover an entire city with a cold blanket of snow and ice! Severe weather comes in many shapes and sizes and can result in dangerous weather for anyone in its path!

Spin-n-Grin

To find the silly answer to the riddle, start at the letter marked with a dot at the top of the tornado. Follow the curving path down to the ground, picking up every third letter as you go.

What is a tornado's favorite party game?

HURRICANES: LARGE AND IN CHARGE

Hurricanes by Any Other Names

Hurricanes are also called typhoons, cyclones, and even willy-willys in other parts of the world!

Longest-Lived Hurricane

In 1899, Hurricane San Ciriaco existed for nearly twenty-eight days, making it the longest-lived hurricane on record. Most hurricanes live for just a week or so.

Picture in your mind a hurricane. What are you seeing? Chances are you're picturing heavy rains, strong winds, or maybe even a large swirling area of clouds with an eye in the center! *Hurricanes* are large areas of low pressure that usually form in the warm, moist air near the equator. They are the largest of severe weather storms, often bigger than many of the states and countries they pass over! They spin, too, like a giant whirlpool in the sky that can stretch over 500 miles from end to end! Hurricanes can produce flooding rains, damaging winds, and large areas of severe weather!

Hurricanes form during a special time, known as hurricane season. For people living in the Northern Hemisphere, hurricane season starts in the summer and lasts until late in autumn. During most other times of the year, conditions are not right for hurricanes to develop. So what does it take to make a hurricane? Just like making a cake, an arts and crafts project, or even a peanut butter and jelly sandwich, you need the right ingredients at just the right time. Hurricane ingredients include warm ocean water temperatures, the correct tilt of the earth on its axis, and special winds and pressure near the spot of hurricane growth. Speaking of growth, what becomes a hurricane must go through stages of growth, starting out as baby-like clusters of storms that mature and change into larger, stronger adult spinning groups of thunderstorms and wind. The process from hurricane birth until hurricane death may take a couple weeks or so! From there, hurricanes can change, grow, and die out over a span of many weeks. And it all starts with warm, moist ocean water near the equator of the earth!

Where would you rather go swimming if you were looking for really warm ocean water, somewhere near the equator or off the coast of Iceland? Hey, nothing against Iceland, but the warmest water will be near the equator. There, during the summer and into the autumn season, the water temperature gets really warm. All of that warm, moist air lifts up into the cooler sky above, forming a large area of thunderstorms known as a *tropical depression*. If the ingredients are right, the storms keep growing and growing until the earth's spin and tilt make them start rotating like a large spinning top. At that point, the system is called a tropical storm with heavy rains, meaning thunderstorms and winds up to about 70 miles per hour. Something else happens at this point of growth: the system is given a name! Storm names are chosen each season by the National Weather Service and are given to tropical storms and hurricanes in alphabetical order throughout the season.

If a tropical storms grows even more powerful and the winds around the storm move the air over 74 miles per hour, a hurricane is born! At that point the storms looks like a large swirling pinwheel of clouds with a dark spot in the center called an *eye*. Around the eye of a hurricane, the strongest winds and rain usually form in an area called the *eye wall*. To better understand a hurricane, picture an adult cutting the grass with a gas-powered lawn mower. As the lawn mover itself moves slowly in a certain direction, the fast-moving blades

Watch Out!

Color in all the letters that are not F, L, or X. Read the answer from left to right, and top to bottom.

What did the boy hurricane say to the girl hurricane?

LFXIXFX
LHXAFV
XEXMFX
YXLEFYL
EFLOFLN
YFXLFOF
FLXUXFL

HURRICANE NAMES

Using all of your friends and family members' names, make a pretend list of hurricane names. Remember, they have to be arranged in alphabetical order and include at least twenty different names, just like the ones listed by the National Weather Service each hurricane season. Who will be the first and last storm of the season on your list?

Wizard of Oz Tornado

Have you seen the movie called *The Wizard of Oz*? That make-believe tornado formed in Kansas, which is right in the middle of Tornado Alley, where most of the tornadoes form in the United States. The one in the movie was built out of a 30-foot-tall piece of rubber!

under it cut the grass and spin around like a pinwheel. Hurricanes move in a similar way, where the whole storm is like the lawn mower moving slowly, and the fast-moving winds around the storms act like the quick-spinning blades, cutting the grass below. Hurricanes can produce dangerous thunderstorms, dump several inches of flooding rain, and produce winds that spin the air over 150 miles per hour, cutting down many objects in their path. Now that's a severe storm!

TORNADOES: SMALL AND OUT OF CONTROL

As you've just learned, hurricanes are often hundreds of miles long and are large enough to cover an entire state or even country! What about the size of a tornado? Picture it in your mind. Compared to a hurricane, a tornado is small, even smaller than your town or even your house! Don't let its small size fool you; the winds and damage caused by a tornado can be much more severe than even the largest hurricane. Tornadoes are violently swirling tubes of air that hang down from storm clouds like dark funnels from the sky. While hurricanes can last a few weeks, tornadoes often last just a few minutes, coming and going before a weather forecast is even made!

Like hurricanes and most other severe storms, tornadoes usually need warm, moist air to grow and develop. When warm, moist air is pushed into a colder air mass, large thunderstorms often form. Such is the case near strong cold fronts that move south from Canada into the United States. Once the two air masses collide, air is twisted and turned in the atmosphere in a way that creates small, fast-moving whirlpools of rotating air in the thunderstorm. If the rotating shafts of fast-moving air in the thunderstorms tilt down from the cloud in just the right way, a funnel appears and extends downward to the ground, forming what we see as a tornado!

To understand how a tornado forms from clashing air currents, try putting a pencil in the palm of your open hand. Now, place your other hand on top of the hand with the pencil and rub your two open hands together with the pencil in the middle of both hands. What is the pencil doing? It's spinning around! That pencil is spinning because each of your hands is forcing the pencil to move in opposite directions. In similar ways, wind currents, called *wind shear*, move air in opposite directions in strong thunderstorms where air masses collide. The spinning pencil is just like the spinning funnel of air that forms a tornado that hangs down from the sky!

You've heard of a bowling alley, right? In a bowling alley, you can find a narrow strip of action where bowling balls and pins are moving and colliding. But have you ever heard of Tornado Alley? *Tornado Alley* is the name given to a strip of flat land in the United States extending from Texas to North Dakota where tornadoes are most common (see the following figure). Over 1,000 tornadoes form in the United States each year, many of them in Tornado Alley, and most of them in the spring and summer months. Think about walking barefoot across a sidewalk on a sunny afternoon. Have you ever noticed how hot your feet can get on a warm summer day as compared with a cool day in autumn? That's because during the spring and summer, the earth's surface (including

Words to Know

wind shear

Wind shear is the change in wind direction and speed in different parts of the atmosphere. Like the blades of scissors moving in opposite directions when they cut paper, wind shear moves air in different directions causing sharp changes in air movement that help tornadoes to form.

the sidewalk you get hot feet from) heats up, causing warm air to rise upward into a cool atmosphere. When cool, dry air from Canada moves south into the warm, moist air near the surface, the air rises up into the sky forming large, powerful thunderstorms, some containing tornadoes. Near Tornado Alley the flat land; warm, moist air from the Gulf of Mexico; and cool, dry air from Canada all work together to make it a special place for tornadoes to grow and spin out of control making more severe weather!

Tornado Alley

THUNDERSTORMS: THE ELECTRICITY IS OUT!

You've seen the flashes of bluish white light on the distant horizon. You've heard the pounding of rain and the blast of thunder rumble through your house. You may have even lost power and electricity to your house because of thunder and lightning! Maybe you've even seen ice fall from the sky on a hot, summer afternoon during a thunderstorm. What exactly is a thunderstorm? How does it produce such weird and scary weather?

Like other forms of severe weather, thunderstorms form when warm, moist air moves up into the sky where it cools, condenses, and forms large, tall cumulonimbus clouds with fast-moving currents of air within them. As a matter of fact, both hurricanes and tornadoes are associated with and form as a part of thunderstorms. What makes thunderstorms so special is that they can produce electricity. Yes, electricity! The same type of stuff flowing as electrical current through the wires in your house and school can also form in the atmosphere near a thunderstorm! And just like the electricity in your home, lightning from a thunderstorm can be very, very dangerous.

To understand how lightning forms, you need to know a little bit about electricity, and also static electricity. Electricity can flow like water in a river in what is called an *electric current*. Electric currents form where there are areas of different charge, like where there are positive and negatively charged areas. When materials rub up against each other, the atoms and particles that make up the material become

MAKE SOME STATIC ELECTRICITY LIGHTNING

By rubbing a balloon against your hair, or your shoes against carpeting, you can create a static electricity charge. Try doing it in a dark room or at night and watch for small flashes of bluish colored light. What you're actually making is a weak flow of electricity or mini-thunderstorm, without the rain and thunder, of course.

F U N F A C T

The Speed of Lightning!

Lightning travels at the speed of light. If it could bend around the earth, the light from lightning would travel around the earth seven times in one second! Now that's fast! In the same amount of time, sound from thunder would only travel about as far as four football fields.

Try This

COUNT TO FIVE!

As soon as you see a flash of lightning from a thunderstorm, start counting in seconds until you hear the sound of the thunder. For every five seconds you count between the seeing the lighting and hearing the thunder, the thunderstorm is one mile away! For example, if you end up counting to ten, the storm is about two miles away.

"upset" from the motion, creating both positive and negatively charged areas. Have you ever rubbed your feet across a carpet and then touched a doorknob? When you do that, you create areas of different charge because of the fast motion of your feet across the atoms that make up the carpet. You may have felt a small shock of static electricity. Now, think of that type of static electricity only much more powerful and in the clouds, without the doorknob!

So what actually does the rubbing motion that makes positive and negative charges to develop in large thunderstorm clouds? It's not a carpet, or fast-moving feet, or even a doorknob, it's water and ice crystals! Remember, in most severe storms, fast-moving currents of air form as cold air collides and mixes with rising, warm, moist air. As that air rises up in the cloud into the cold sky above, ice crystals form, collide, and mix together like the movements in a large blender. With all of that rubbing and colliding of ice particles, areas of positive and negative charge form in the cloud. When the charge difference between the thunderstorm cloud and the ground below becomes great enough, electricity breaks out in what you see and hear as a stroke of lightning!

The Sights and Sounds of a Thunderstorm

The sky lights up, the windows shake, and the booms of thunder echo across the land. Just what happens when static electricity in the form of lightning from a thunderstorm rips through the sky? The temperature of the air near the actual lightning bolt heats up to over 20,000°F! The air gets so hot in a short period of time that it expands outward producing the loud sound we hear as thunder! The light from the lightning travels much faster than the sound from thunder, so you never really get both thunder and lightning at the same time. Often, the thunder from a distant thunderstorm never actually reaches your ears, and all you can see is the light from

ZAP ZAP ZAPPITY ZAP

In July of 2008, severe thunderstorms pounded western Washington state. While the thunder, wind, and rain were bad enough, the lightning was incredible! Do the math to learn how many lightning strikes were estimated for the time period of Wednesday afternoon through Thursday morning. If you think the answer you get is amazing, think about this—thunderstorms were predicted to continue for another whole day!

Add up the number of...

...days in two years   _____

...sheets of paper in a ream   _____

...pennies in $10   _____

...cookies in 20 dozen   _____

...toes on three people   _____

This is the total number of lightning strikes estimated in western Washington state during this one day!

the lightning far, far away. On a dark night, you can actually see a thunderstorm's lightning from as far as 50 miles away or more, but you might not hear a single rumble of thunder from it. The light from the lightning can reach your eyes, but the sound of thunder can't reach your ears!

SNOWSTORMS: SCHOOL IS OUT!

Snowstorm! Just reading it and saying it makes many kids think of fun stuff. Maybe the word makes you think of having school off. Or does it make you think of playing outside in the snow all day, building snowmen, sleigh riding, and skiing? Snowstorms can be fun, but they can also be very dangerous. Cars off roads, people stranded in homes or buildings, dangerous winds, blinding white-out conditions, and everything and everyone stopped in their tracks! Yes, snow can be fun, but the storms that produce snow can create weather so dangerous that some snowstorms can be called severe, much like hurricanes, tornadoes, and thunderstorms. If you live in a mountainous area, or northern part of the United States, chances are you've been through a few snowstorms. Think about all of the things that happened during the last snowstorm you can remember!

Like other severe storms, special ingredients must come together for snowstorms to form. Unlike other types of severe storms, snowstorms don't need as much moist air and warm temperatures to help get them going. Most snowstorms are very strong areas of low pressure that form during the cold season in many parts of the world. Remember, when air is lifted up into the sky, it cools and condenses into clouds and precipitation. Think of a low-pressure area and a snowstorm

No Two Snowflakes Alike?

Did you ever hear someone say that no two snowflakes are alike? As water freezes to make ice crystals and snowflakes, it produces millions and billions of different shapes and sizes of snowflakes. However, if you really looked closely at enough of them, you would find many look so alike you could say they are twins.

as a large vacuum cleaner that sucks air (not carpet dust) up into the great hose in the sky. Because so much air is sucked up, the air pressure is usually very low around snowstorms. As the air pressure gets lower, the winds blow stronger! So, snowstorms are usually associated with areas of low pressure and fast-moving wind speeds, but what else? For a lot of snow to fall, there must be enough moisture to make snow and enough cold air to keep the moisture as snow.

Most snowstorms in the United States form during the months of December, January, February, and March. During those months, the jet stream is very active with dips, dives, curves, moisture, and cold and warm air masses on the move. Remember, a big dip or downward bend in the jet steam is called a trough. Most snowstorms form as a part of a

WHICH ONE?

Which word is often used to describe powerful snowstorms with strong winds that form mainly along the East Coast of the United States.

1. Monsoon
2. Doldrums
3. Westerly
4. Nor'easter

4. Nor'easter

Snowstorm Jet Map

Jet Stream

COLD

L

Mild Pacific Air

Southern Jet Stream

Snow Day

Kids who live where it snows get a day off from school when the flakes pile up. But in April, 1921, the kids of Silver Lake, Colorado, got a super snow day! The National Climate Extremes Committee has this city on record for the most snow to fall in 24 hours. Do the math and see how many feet of snow Silver Lake got.

Rate of Snowfall
3.15
inches per hour

That's not much!

1. How many inches of snow fell in 24 hours?

That's more like it!

Multiply rate of snowfall by 24.

2. How many feet of snow fell in 24 hours?

YIKES!

Divide answer to question one by 12.

large jet steam trough. In the trough, cold temperatures bend south, while on the right side (or east) of the trough, warmer air moves up from the south. Snowstorms and strong low-pressure areas often form where the cold and warm air meet on the right (east) side of the jet stream trough. Look at the preceding diagram and notice how the jet stream is forming a large trough, low-pressure area (snowstorm), and warm and cold air movements.

In many snowstorms, the coldest air, greatest wind, and most snow will form on the northern and western side of a low-pressure area, just like on the map. Think of a snowstorm low-pressure area as a giant clock. The snowiest weather is usually near the spots where the numbers 7, 8, 9, 10, 11, and 12 are located on the face of the clock.

On the warmer side of the low-pressure area, where the numbers 1, 2, 3, 4, 5, and 6 are on a clock, it may be a normal rainy day! Remember, it's just a low-pressure area, like so many others that produce rainy days and cloudy skies. It's all about the snow. Snow is made up of tiny little balls or crystals of ice. Snow is slippery, cold, and gets in the way of our modern lives. So when the jet steam is just right, the temperatures cold enough, and a low-pressure area is in just the right spot heading your way, watch out! The snow may be piling up outside your house, around your town, and near your school! You may be in for a snowstorm!

CHAPTER 8

Light Shows in the Sky

WHY IS THE SKY BLUE AND RED?

Why are leaves green? Why are T-shirts white? Why are apples red? Why is dirt brown? Why is the sky blue? At this point, a better question is what is color? Light from bright objects like the sun, a light bulb, the moon, or a flashlight is made up of many different types of energy. What we see as light is really made up of energetic waves of energy called *radiation*. Hey, I know it sounds dangerous, but radiation is everywhere. Heat, light, television, radio, and cell phone signals are just a few examples of the different types of radiation. It's all around you right now as you read this sentence. This very book is producing heat radiation and reflecting light radiation. One of the things that make one type of radiation different from another is something called the *wavelength*.

The colors of light you see with your eyes are really just different types of waves and wavelengths coming from different objects. The seven main colors of light (radiation) or wave-

Words to Know

wavelength

The wavelength is the distance from crest to crest or hump to hump of a wave. Just like ripples in a puddle of water or waves on the ocean, most waves look like squiggly lines. Some have large wavelengths and some have short wavelengths.

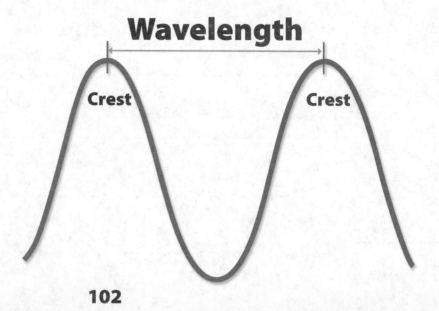

Wavelength

Crest

Crest

lengths are red, orange, yellow, green, blue, indigo, and violet. You can remember the seven main colors by the make-believe name ROY G BIV. When all of those colors or wavelengths, known as the visible spectrum, are mixed together, your eyes see the color white. Most T-shirts are white because the material that makes up the shirt reflects the seven colors of ROY G BIV all back to your eyes. Dirt appears black or dark brown in color because it does not reflect much of the visible spectrum back to your eyes, so what you see is "missing" wavelengths of color, or dark brown and black. What makes objects have what we call color is how much of the visible spectrum is reflected and absorbed by the object.

So, why is the sky blue? Actually, it's seen in many different colors! At night the sky is black! With no sunlight, the air and atmosphere above simply does not reflect or absorb any of the visible spectrum. Since you are not getting any light color or radiation to your eyes, you don't see any color at all, which is the color black! During the daytime, the sun's light (ROY G BIV) floods the atmosphere, which is filled with atoms and molecules of air. Because of the longer red, orange, yellow, and green wavelengths, the molecules of air absorb most of those colors. That leaves the blues and violets. These BIVs are scattered around by the air, reflecting it back to your eyes, while the ROY Gs never make it. The blue sky is really just the shorter wavelengths of blue, indigo, and violet making it all the way from the sun to your eyeballs. Most of ROY G just can't make it through the atmosphere! Hello BIV!

Have you ever seen the sky turn a bright orange, pink, or reddish color? It's a beautiful sight that is most often seen in the morning or evening near sunrise and sunset. To understand why the atmosphere can turn red, imagine sticking your finger in a shallow puddle of water. If you stick your finger straight in and straight down in the water, only the tip of your finger is actually in the puddle. Now imagine

Try This

MAKE A ROY G BIV SPECTRUM

Using crayons, water paint, or colored pencils, create a strip of different colors in the order of red, orange, yellow, green, blue, indigo, and violet. You will end up with a scientific display of color in order of wavelength as they appear in nature, called the visible spectrum!

sticking your finger in the puddle from the side, or at a tilt. Now, more of your finger is actually in the puddle of water. Sunlight acts just like your finger and the atmosphere just like the puddle of water. When the sun is out in the afternoon, it's like your finger straight up in the puddle. The sunlight passes directly into the atmosphere, scattering out the blue, indigo, and violet. When the sun is low in the sky, like during sunrise and sunset, sunlight passes through the puddle of air (atmosphere) from the side, tilted like the finger in the puddle. Because the light (ROY G BIV) is passing through more air (like more of your finger in the puddle at a tilt), more colors are absorbed by the air until only the reds and oranges make it through to your eyes. So you see the sky lit up with the beautiful colors of red and orange!

Light Maze

Find your way from START to END.

START

END

RAINBOWS AND SNOWBOWS?

If you're like most kids, you've probably been drawing rainbows since you were very young. You've probably been drawing them wrong all those years! Try drawing one now. This time, when you draw the rainbow, remember, it must include ROY G BIV. Yes, those colors, in that order! A rainbow arch should have the color red on the outside and violet (purple) on the inside. Remember longer waves first; red, orange, yellow, green in the middle, then blue, indigo, and finally violet. It's science! It has to be that way, but why? How does the atmosphere make rainbows? Why do they often form after or before it rains? And, can snow make snowbows just like rain makes rainbows?

Do you remember what light is made up of? Light radiation energy is made up of the colors ROY G BIV, all mixing together in what we see as white light. To see a color of light, it must be separated from the group. To see all of the colors separated and spread out into a rainbow takes something called *refraction*. Light refraction means to slow down and bend! To understand refraction, think of what happens when you throw a rock really fast into a lake. When the rock hits the water, it slows down and changes the direction it was moving before it hit the water. You can say the rock refracted! When light hits drops of water in clouds or in raindrops, it also slows down, changes it direction, and bends, or refracts.

Each color of light (ROY G BIV) bends and refracts in a different way. The ROYs bend a little less that the BIVs, so the colors end up spreading out in what we see as a rainbow. It's like the rock that was thrown into the lake broke up into

RAINBOWS AND WRONGBOWS?

Look through some books, magazines, and drawings and see if you can find rainbows. Then, see if they are drawn correctly. Remember, rainbows should be made up of ROY G BIV colors in that order from the outside to the inside of the bow. Many books and images of rainbows are WRONGBOWS that really don't exist!

REFRACTION IN A GLASS OF WATER

Fill a small-sized drinking glass with water almost to the top. Next, place a pencil in the glass of water and allow about half of the pencil to stick out of the water. Now look at the pencil from the side. It appears to bend in the water! The light from the pencil is refracting or bending in the water just like light bends in raindrops that form rainbows!

smaller pieces, and each piece moved a different way as it sank to the bottom. Remember, when light refracts, it bends, and when light bends its colors, they all separate out in what you see as the rainbow of ROY G BIV. So to make a rainbow, all you need is sunlight, drops of water in the sky from a distant rain shower, and, of course, someone in the right place to see the light that gets bent and refracted from the drops!

The light from a rainbow travels from the sun to drops in the clouds to your eyes. Yes, your eyes! Someone looking at a rainbow right next to you is actually seeing light from the sun going through different drops to *her* eyes. They may look the same, but no two people really see the same rainbow! In the same way, there is really no end to a rainbow. Remember, it's just light being bent from drops in the clouds. If you were to try and follow or chase a rainbow, you would never see its end. You would end up just seeing misty drops in the air as the light from the sun gets bent to someone else far, far away! It's all just an illusion of light in the sky.

Snowbows?

If rain drops and rain can make rainbows, then why can't snow make snowbows? Remember what happens when sunlight enters raindrops: it bends and refracts, just like a rock slows down and changes direction when it is thrown into a lake. Now, imagine what would happen if you threw that same rock onto the lake when the water was frozen. Would the rock refract and bend into the ice, or would it bounce off of it? The rock would most likely bounce right of the ice! When light from the sun passes onto snowflakes in the sky, most of the light bounces off of the snowflake, just like the rock off of the ice. Without refraction or bending, ROY G BIV just can't bee seen. No refraction, no bending, no SNOWBOW!

RAINBOWS EVERYWHERE!

Remember, whenever light bends or refracts it may form a rainbow of color. Think of different places where you may have seen rainbows form. Make a list of some of those places. Examples of places you can see rainbows include CDs, oil spills, windows, misty garden hose sprays, waterfalls, and so on.

Bow Wow

Once in a while there is a strange pattern of light in the sky. Two colorful, shiny spots show up on either side of the sun, at the same height. They are caused by light bouncing through ice crystals high in the atmosphere. The scientific name for one of these spots is a "parhelic circle." To learn the common name, connect the dots!

THERE'S A RING AROUND THE SUN!

The atmosphere can produce so many different displays of light. From electric blue skies to red sunsets to the spectrum of the rainbow, the sky above can make some unique sights and colors. One of the weirder weather sights you can observe in the sky is a large ring or circle around the sun and moon. Yes, a perfect circle of light, like a full rainbow, as if it were drawn on paper, with the moon or sun placed in the center like art work! Why would this weather art form in the sky? Why a ring? What does it mean? In past human history, a ring around the sun or moon was often seen as a sign or warning that something bad was about to happen. Even today if you see a ring around the sun and moon, a storm system often arrives a day or two later. Yes, a ring in the sky can help you forecast rain and snow! What could it all mean?

It all starts with cirrus clouds. Remember from Chapter 3 that cirrus clouds are high, thin clouds that are made up of tiny little pieces and crystals of ice. Think of them as little chunks of broken pieces of glass that form over three miles above your head! Even on a hot summer day, it's so cold at that height that ice crystals can still form in the clouds. When cirrus clouds cover the sky and thicken, they are called *cirrostratus clouds*. Just think, on certain days the only "large" objects between your eyes and the sun millions of miles away may be ice crystals from cirrostratus clouds! When sunlight tries to pass through these clouds, the tiny ice crystals in the cloud slow the light down and bend it in different ways. The bent light shoots out of the clouds and back to the earth, but not in a straight path. The bending of light coming from the sun by ice crystals in clouds changes

Try This

BENDING LIGHT WITH A DROP OF WATER

Gently place a drop of water onto printed words from a newspaper, magazine, or old book. Make sure the drop of water stays in the form of a ball or at least a flattened ball. Notice how the letters in the words look through the drop. The light passing through the drop of water makes the letters look stretched and weird. Try the same thing with an ice cube. That's what happens to light as it passes through clouds!

the path of light, which you see as a halo or ring around the moon or sun.

To understand the ring a little better, imagine you are a ray of light from the sun. On most days, you would take a straight path from the sun to the earth! Now, imagine you are a ray of light from the sun passing through ice crystals in cirrus clouds. On your way through the ice, your path is bent, and you don't go in a straight line like the other rays of light but bend off to the side. It's that bending of light, millions and millions of times by millions and millions of ice crystals, that produces the bright ring of light seen around the sun and moon. Look at the diagram below and notice how light is changed as it passes through ice in clouds.

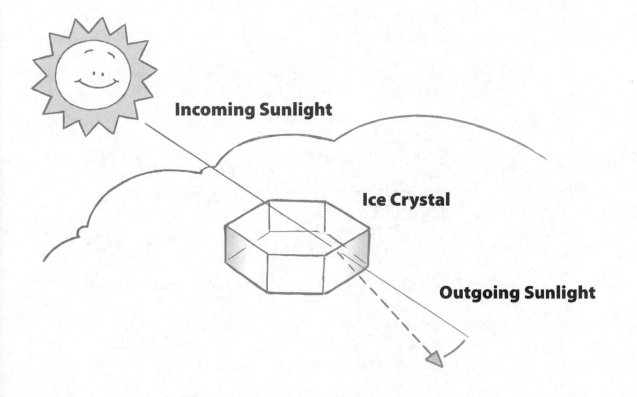

Incoming Sunlight

Ice Crystal

Outgoing Sunlight

Usually a day or two after a ring is seen around the sun or moon, rain or snow and a storm system will move in! Why would a ring in the clouds have anything to do the making of a storm and precipitation? It's not so much the ring but the type of clouds that form the ring that can be used to forecast a storm. Cirrus and cirrostratus clouds usually form when warmer air is being pushed into colder air from hundreds of miles away! If you remember from Chapter 5, the warmer air rides up over the colder air and forms an area of condensation, clouds, and precipitation near a weather system known as a warm front. As the warmer air rides up and over the colder air, cirrus clouds form high in the sky, hundreds of miles before the warm front. The cirrus clouds that help make the halo or ring usually become lower and thinner as the warm front gets closer. Also, cirrus clouds (and rings) can often form before and ahead of some thunderstorms and hurricanes. So the next time you see a ring around the sun or moon, think about cirrus clouds, ice crystals, and the bending of light, but also get your umbrella or snow shovel ready, because a storm is probably heading your way!

WHAT'S A PUDDLE DOING ON THE HIGHWAY? MIRAGES

Imagine yourself on a warm sunny day, looking down a road or highway. You notice the cars whizzing by, the blue sky, and the flat, long, dark-colored blacktop baking in the sun. What's that up ahead? It looks like a puddle of water or pond has formed in the middle of the road. But it can't be. It hasn't rained, and it's a hot, dry day! Have you ever seen what looks like a puddle of water on a hot, dry road surface? What could it be? To make things even more interesting, if you chase down and try to find the "puddle" on the road, it disappears! In a way, you've been tricked by the workings of light, heat, and air. What you see on the road is not real! Or is it? It's a mirage!

A mirage is an illusion! It is something you think you are seeing that really isn't there. Most magic acts and magicians use illusions to trick your eyes into seeing things that you really are not seeing. A mirage on a hot road can form right before your eyes and make you think you are seeing a puddle of water on the road when you really are not! To understand how a mirage forms, think about what happens when you look in the mirror. Is that really you in the mirror? There is only ONE you! When you look into a mirror, you are seeing light from your body being reflected and bent back to your eyes. It looks like you, but it's really just light from your body being bent and bounced back at you! When mirages form, like a puddle on the road or an oasis in a desert, it's really just light bouncing and bending around, making you see things that are not real.

Have you ever tried to walk barefoot over beach sand or on a blacktop driveway on a hot, sunny day? Ouch! On a hot, sunny day, the sun's light warms the earth's surface. Some surfaces, like blacktop and sand, warm up faster than other surfaces like grass or dirt. You can actually see how the sun's light energy changes the air and temperature near the ground, making it look blurry and wavy as the heat builds. It's that heated air near the hotter ground that can also bend light. As the light from nearby objects bends and changes direction, you see things differently. What you see is an illusion, or a mirage.

Try This

WHAT'S HOTTER, BLACK OR WHITE?

On a warm, sunny day, place one thermometer under a sheet of white paper and the other under a sheet of black paper. After about 10 to 15 minutes, check the temperature of both thermometers. Which thermometer has the highest reading? The black sheet of paper will absorb more sunlight and warm up faster, just like a highway heats up faster on a warm, sunny day, which helps to form mirages and bend light.

The puddle of water that you can see near the hot road surface is an illusion. It looks blue like water and it even seems to move around like water does, but it is just a mirage. The puddle of blue that you see is actually light bent from the blue sky above! In much the same way that water, mirrors, and other substances can change sunlight's path, heated air can bend it, too. Light from the sky above is actually bent to your eyes by the heated air near the road surface forming the illusion of water on the road! A similar mirage can form from hot sand on a beach or in the desert. Instead of seeing a puddle of blue water on the road, an oasis of water can appear in a dry, barren desert. But it is just an illusion. There is no water or puddle, just light from the sky bouncing and bending around in the air on a hot summer day!

Sky Lights

Subject words from this chapter are each hidden three times in the puzzle grids.

RAINBOW   RING   HALO   STARS   MIRAGE   ICE

```
F V G N I R S    E I F    O V K Y    R S F    B V E
R F T O E P V    G S P    F I W    I I O    H O J
T A V C    A F O    I T O P    C N P V A F
O P I I    R V I    O B I    E N G S L J
F S O N P F V    I F O    N O P    F W T O
  T S B T P    M P L I F S    M O F S
  R P O O F    I T A F P S V    I B S T
F O A F V L P W    P R H P V T F J    R N V A
I T T P A O I P    F O S    T A O I    A I O R
S P O H P S F T    I C E    O R I N G    G A T S
P E G A R I M I    K V P    S K P K J    E R F V
```

NORTHERN LIGHTS AND METEOR SHOWERS

Now that you've learned so much about light shows in the sky, think about all of the different colors that you can see in the sky. The atmosphere is filled with all the colors of the rainbow, from the reds of sunset to the everyday bright blue sky! Even at night, the dark sky has its own blackness that is like nothing else. You've learned how light can be bent, slowed down, twisted, and bounced around to form more colors in the sky than are in your crayon box. But there are a few more natural light shows that are common on the earth that are not from the bending of light. No drops of rain or ice crystals are needed, nor bouncing of sunlight, either. Some of these light shows involve the activity of "visitors" from outside of the earth's atmosphere, and they are coming in right now! Millions and millions of them are passing through the atmosphere and lighting up the sky! They are meteors and high-speed particles from space that often cause the atmosphere to glow!

Most stars are much larger than our entire planet and never shoot across the sky!

To understand what meteors are and how they can put on a light show, you must know a little bit about the "stuff" of space. You may already know about stuff like planets, asteroids, and stars, but think of all of the smaller stuff. Think of it as dust and dirt! Space is loaded with it, from tiny chunks of rock and metal to material smaller than grains of sand and chalk dust. As the earth orbits the sun, it moves around in a large circular pattern like cars around a race track. And

FUN FACT
Shooting Stars!

Have you every seen a shooting star? That is a name given to what is really a meteor. Most meteors that you see streak across the sky are smaller than a grain of sand!

Try This

METEOR COUNT!

On any clear night, ask your parents to take you to a dark place away from city lights, cars, and street lights. With a blanket under you, lie down flat on your back and just stare up into the night sky. If you're patient enough, you should be able to see a few meteors steak across the sky. Count how many you can see in a half-hour. How about an hour! Don't fall asleep!

F U N F A C T

Fluorescent Lights and Northern Lights

Fluorescent lights are made from long glass tubes that have special air inside them and coatings on the glass. When electricity is added to them, the particles inside become "excited" and glow and produce light in the same way that the air glows above the North and South Poles of the earth from the solar wind!

just like cars will often run into a cloud of dust smoke on the track, the earth passes through some big clouds of dust and gas in space. Once this material is pulled into the earth's atmosphere by gravity, it begins to speed up and get very hot as it travels toward the surface of our planet. It's happening all of the time, like right now! At night, you can look up and watch some of the material burn up in the sky. What you can see is a streak of light that moves across the sky, usually lasting only a second or two. That's what we call a meteor. On nearly any night of the year, if you look up on a clear night, you can watch them streak across the sky. On some nights, you can see just a few each hour. During special nights, when space is really dusty, you can see a hundreds of meteors streak across the sky each hour! Now that's a cool light show.

Most meteors that you can see in the sky are burning up miles above your head. If a meteor starts out very large, it may actually make it all the way to the earth's surface before burning up! When the object makes it all the way to the ground, it's then called a *meteorite*! The roof of your house and the surface of the earth are often covered with tiny meteorite dust! Some meteorites are as big as pebbles and stones. Even larger ones have struck the earth in the past. Some meteorites have been so large that they have left craters that are many miles wide and hundreds of feet deep on the surface of the earth! It is believed that a meteorite or similar object struck the earth over 65 million years ago, causing major changes that led to the extinction of many forms of life including the dinosaurs. Imagine what a spectacular light show that meteor produced in the atmosphere before it collided with our planet!

There are even smaller visitors from space that pass into our atmosphere and put on lightshows. Particles much smaller than meteor dust constantly pound our air from above. The particles are coming from the sun and are called the *solar wind*. The solar wind "blows" out from the sun and is made up of charged particles from atoms making up the sun. Atoms are one of the smallest and most basic forms of matter that make up everything, even the sun. When the solar wind particles reach the earth, they gather near the North and South Poles of our planet. Imagine all of those particles and energy being pumped into the sky above the North and South Poles. What does it do to the air there? People who live in the northern and southern parts of the earth often see the sky above glow in multicolored curtains of light called the northern (and southern) lights!

Because the sun is more active during some years compared to others, the solar wind changes from year to year. When the solar wind is strong, the sky above the North and South Poles begins to glow even more from the added energy. The night sky turns into dancing colors of blue, green, red, and yellow from all of the excitement. It's eerie and cool to watch the colors of light come and go across long nights and cold sky over the South and North Poles of our planet!

Words to Know

aurora borealis

The northern lights are also called the aurora borealis. They are called the northern lights because they form over the northern parts of the earth and can only be seen in the northern part of the sky! In the Southern Hemisphere the opposite is true, and they are called the southern lights or aurora australis.

CHAPTER 9

What Does a Meteorologist Do?

WEATHER STATIONS

What does it really mean to be a meteorologist? Where does a meteorologist work? What does a meteorologist do? You know that doctors and nurses work in hospitals, and that teachers and students work in school buildings. But did you know that most meteorologists work in a special place called a weather station? Think about the kinds of things that a meteorologist must have to study the weather. A meteorologist must be able to get and gather weather information, forecast the weather, and then get all of the weather information out to the people who need it! A weather station is a really neat place with many maps, displays, computers, and special instruments placed outside and inside that tell a meteorologist what is going on in the air and atmosphere.

Most weather stations have weather instruments placed outside that first tell meteorologists what is going on at that moment in the air around the instruments. Many of these important weather readings come from instruments placed in a special box called an *instrument shelter*. Think of it as a little weather hut. Instrument shelters protect thermometers and humidity instruments from the sun, rain, and snow while still allowing them to be outside in the weather. Wind speed and direction are also measured at most weather stations. A special weather instrument, called an *anemometer*, spins around like a sideways windmill that moves faster and faster as the winds blows to measure wind speed. A *wind vane* looks like an arrow that points into the direction that the wind is coming from and measures wind direction. Many weather stations have anemometers and wind vanes high up on a pole or mast, where the wind is not affected by buildings and trees. Following is a diagram showing an instrument shelter, wind vane, and anemometer as they would be seen at many weather stations.

TAKE A TOUR OF A WEATHER STATION!

Would you like to see a real weather station? Most television stations, colleges, and airports have weather stations that offer tours to the public. Ask a parent, teacher, or group leader to call up and arrange a tour of a weather station. Take a camera along, you'll be seeing a lot of exciting stuff!

Another important part of a weather station is the measurement of rain and snow. Meteorologists, gardeners, farmers, and many people who work outdoors need to know how much rain falls from the sky! To measure precipitation, meteorologists use a special instrument called a *rain gauge*. Most rain gauges are simply containers placed outside in an open area away from trees and buildings. Usually, a larger opening funnels the rain down into a smaller opening where measurements are made by a meteorologist. Even snowfall

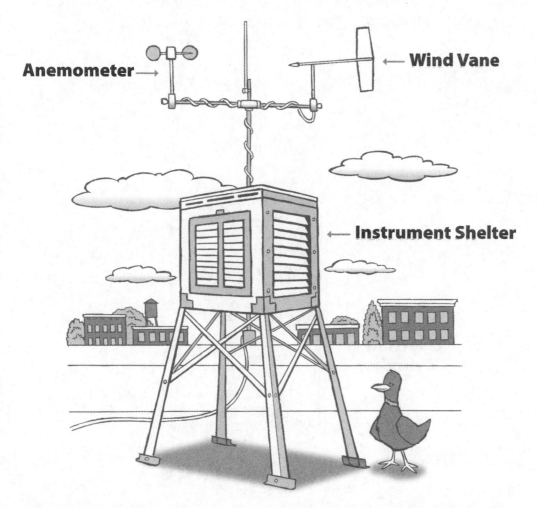

Anemometer →

Wind Vane ←

← **Instrument Shelter**

measurements must be done in a special way at weather stations. Have you ever tried to measure snow near your house? You will find that how much snow piles up on the ground is affected by the wind, the temperature of the surface that the snow is falling on, and what's nearby as you measure. A meteorologist's snow measurement is often made on a special surface, in an open area that is not affected by blowing and drifting. Yes, even snowfall is serious business at a weather station.

The most important part of most weather stations is the meteorologist. Meteorologists and weather experts can see,

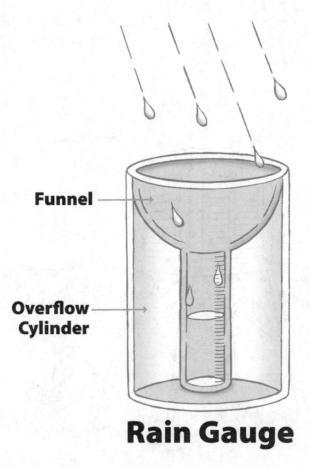

Funnel

Overflow Cylinder

Rain Gauge

feel, observe, and record weather information and report it to other weather stations all over the earth. However, some weather stations are in spots that are hard to get to or do not need a meteorologist at the site. How would you like to go outside and check the weather instruments on top of a cold, windy mountain, or in the middle of an ocean or desert? For those and other areas of harsh weather, many of the weather stations are now automated. The word *automated* means to work automatically, without the need for humans. Automated weather stations have special instruments on them that record and gather weather conditions without the help of human beings or meteorologists. They record temperature, wind, barometer, and rainfall information with their computers and instruments. Meteorologists use the information from these weather stations to better understand how the weather is acting in areas where meteorologists are not available. In recent years, many of these weather stations have been placed at airports, schools, and even at sea! No matter how the information is gathered, it is very important for meteorologists to first know what is happening outside. Weather stations do just that and much more!

Try This

MAKE A RAIN GAUGE

Ask your parents for an empty soup or coffee can or plastic container with straight sides and one open end. Place it outside, away from trees and buildings, before it rains. With the help of your family, simply measure the water inside with a ruler to see how much rain has fallen. Most rain storms produce less that one inch of rainfall. How much will you get?

COMPUTERS, SATELLITES, AND FORECASTING TOOLS

Think about how meteorology has changed since your parents or grandparents were born. They may seem old to you, but it's really not too long ago when they were your age and meteorology was very different from today. Just fifty years ago, there were no weather satellites in space. When you watch weather forecasts on television today, you probably don't think much about how you can see storms and clouds from space. That wasn't possible until recent years! There were no real computers before your parents' time, either! Many of the computers in homes and offices today did not exist just thirty years ago. Today, meteorologists use weather satellites and computers to help them with most of their weather information and forecasting. Let's see how!

What would be the best way for you to watch a sporting event? How could you really see all of the players and watch them move around and interact with each other? Would you like to see it from the sidelines or float above the game like a bird? The best place to see all of the action is from above! Weather satellites do just that for meteorologists. Weather satellites are placed above the earth's atmosphere, constantly taking pictures of clouds, storms, and weather patterns below! Meteorologists watch and study all of the pictures taken by weather satellites and get a look at how weather systems move and change from place to place. Just like a football player running downfield in the direction of the touchdown, meteorologists can track storms, the jet stream, high-pressure systems, and the flow of air across the earth below. They can then predict where the weather systems will be going and who's in their path!

Another important tool meteorologists use in forecasting the weather is Doppler radar. As you read in Chapter 6, radar is a word that stands for RAdio Detection And Ranging. It's a way of bouncing waves of radio energy off of rain and snow in clouds and picking up the echo that comes back. *Doppler radar* equipment is then used to create maps of where areas of rain and snow are, where they're going, and at what speed they're moving. With Doppler radar, meteorologists can even measure how fast the drops of rain in the cloud are moving,

How High Up Is a Weather Satellite?

Most weather satellites stay above the same spot over the earth while constantly taking pictures of the atmosphere below. To do this, they must be placed about 22,000 miles up in orbit around the earth. That's about one tenth of the way to the moon!

which can help predict where strong storms and tornadoes may be forming!

Another helpful tool meteorologists use in weather forecasting is a computer, which can be used to program a computer model of the weather. To understand how computers help forecast the weather, think about how you sometimes play pretend games to see how something would feel. Maybe you pretended you were a professional baseball or football player. How about pretending to be a doctor or ballerina? Meteorologists play pretend with something called a computer model. Computer models show what storms and winds will be like in the future as they "pretend" to be the real weather. Meteorologists use real information from weather observations and then create a pretend weather pattern inside of a computer. The computer model can then be used to help predict what the weather will be like in the future. Meteorologists use many different types of computers and computer models. Often the computer models don't agree, or they give forecasts that end up being wrong! It's up to the meteorologist to try and use his best judgment along with some help from the computers to make a forecast that is the correct one! If the forecast is wrong, computers can take part of the blame, but the meteorologist gets most of it!

F U N F A C T

The Word Doppler

The word *Doppler* comes from Christian Doppler, an Austrian scientist who lived in the 1800s and studied how waves move and change. Most television weather forecasts use Doppler radar systems.

CAREERS IN METEOROLOGY

So you love the weather! You like watching clouds, following weather patterns, and even forecasting the weather just like the meteorologists on television. Maybe you're even thinking of making your own home weather station and someday

Jackpot

Use the decoder to figure out the silly answer to this rainy day riddle!

Why did the silly kid go outside with an empty piggy bank?

A — coin
E — cloud
I — sun
O — raindrops
U — pig

B🌥C🪙🐷S🌥
(BECAUSE)

TH🌥
(THE)

M🌥T🌥💧R💧L💧G☀S T
(METEOROLOGIST)

PR🌥D☀CT🌥D
(PREDICTED)

S💧M🌥　CH🪙NG🌥
(SOME CHANGE)

☀N　TH🌥
(IN THE)

W🌥🪙TH🌥R!
(WEATHER!)

turning a hobby into a career as a real meteorologist! What should you do? How do you do it? Can you do it? If you ask many meteorologists when they first thought about a career in meteorology, they will tell you it first started when they were kids. If it's something you really love, and really work hard at, you too could be a professional weather scientist—a meteorologist!

Like most sciences, meteorology requires a lot of learning and understanding of how things work. If you really enjoy science and math subjects, study hard, do well in school, and then decide to move on to college, you can choose to study meteorology. Most meteorologists have four-year degrees from the many colleges and universities that offer it as a program of study. Once you graduate from college with a meteorology degree, you can then search for ways to use your skills and knowledge of weather and the earth's atmosphere. Remember, not all meteorologists are weather forecasters. A meteorologist is a person who studies the earth's weather, from chasing tornadoes to understanding global warming. It's all about what you really love to do and how you want to use your skills!

Many meteorologists use their skills to forecast the weather. Think of some of the places where a weather forecast is needed. Airports need meteorologists for scheduling their flights. Ski resorts need forecasts for making snow, planning activities, and maintaining trails. Construction businesses and builders need meteorologists to provide accurate forecasts to plan their outdoor activities. Television and radio stations need meteorologists to provide weather forecasts to their viewers and listeners. Vacationers and shoppers need to know when the best time is for their weather-related plans. Even moms, dads, and kids need weather information to plan their day. Just about everyone needs weather forecasts!

FUN FACT

Meteorology Degrees

In the United States there are over 100 different colleges and universities that offer degrees in the atmospheric sciences. Most states have at least one!

Meteorologists work for many of these groups and organizations. Even the government of the United States has meteorologists to help keep their citizens informed of what the weather is doing and what it will do in the future. Meteorologists are needed by just about everyone who steps outside and needs to know what is happening and what will happen! Meteorology is a science that is everywhere and is important to everyone!

Are you hooked yet? Do you want to forecast the weather and inform thousands of people what the atmosphere is doing and what's going to happen in the future? Maybe not! Many meteorologists spend their time not forecasting the weather but studying it to better understand how it works. Some meteorologists spend their time studying global warming and how our planet's weather is changing. Others spend their whole career studying how the weather was in the past, millions of years ago! Still other meteorologists study pollution, rainfall, pollen, drought, flooding, and how weather affects human health and the environment. Some meteorologists end up making more meteorologists by teaching the science of weather to students in high school and college! What all meteorologists have in common is a love for the science of our atmosphere—how it works, how it changes, and how to help other people understand it better! Are you ready for a career in meteorology?

Try This

WHY DO PEOPLE WATCH?

Ask members of your family and friends why they watch the news on television. Research has found that the main reason people watch their local news is to get the weather. See if that's the main reason the people you know watch! Weather is very important!

BEHIND THE SCENES OF A TV METEOROLOGIST

If you ask your parents and friends to name your school's principal, they probably will know it. What about the governor of your state? Would most people be able to name the mayor of your town? How about the star in a Hollywood movie? There are plenty of people that everyone seems to know because they see them everyday or watch them on TV or in a movie. Would your relatives and friends be able to tell you their favorite weatherperson? Just about everyone knows a TV meteorologist! Most people watch them every day and get important information about the weather from them. What exactly do they do? How does a meteorologist do what you see on TV? Who is your favorite meteorologist?

Most television meteorologists or weather forecasters are a very important part of the local news during the morning, noon, evening, and nighttime broadcasts. Remember, your local news and weather is seen by many thousands of people who live in the towns and cities near your home. During the newscast, a meteorologist usually gets only about 3 to 5 minutes to tell everyone around your area what is happening with the weather and what will happen in the future. That's a lot of information in a very short period of time! It's much like making a meal. Often it takes hours of preparation, then just a few minutes of "eating" the meal. Before you even see a meteorologist on television in your local news, she is very busy preparing the weather forecast.

What's involved in making a weather forecast? Meteorologists arrive at work, usually about an hour or two before they present their forecast in the news. In that time, they

Try This

A MAKE-BELIEVE NEWSCAST

With the help of your family and friends, make a local newscast from your house! Use boxes, markers, crayons, and maps to create the set. Have each person play a different newscaster (sports, news, and weather) and make up some local news. Of course, the forecast can be real!

F U N F A C T

The Life of a TV Weather Forecaster

Even though you only see most weather forecasters on television for a few minutes during a newscast, most work eight-hour shifts just like most other people. Many spend their work time making the forecast, studying the weather patterns, and even visiting with groups and organizations.

are busy looking at weather maps, studying the weather patterns, and seeing what is happening with the atmosphere. They watch the pattern of the jet stream, storms, where fronts are, and how weather systems are moving and changing. Computers and computer models help meteorologists decide how weather systems will be moving and what the atmosphere will look like in the future. They also must get a good look at what the current weather is in their forecast area and understand how temperatures, winds, rain, and snowfall amounts will be changed by mountains, rivers, lakes, the ocean, and the environment in the forecast area! Remember, a lot of preparation and science goes into each forecast before you even see it on your television or computer! But it's all fun, too!

Is it time for the forecast yet? Not really! Now that the meteorologist has studied the weather pattern, gathered all of the information, and made up a forecast, he must get ready to show it all off to those watching! Imagine you just came back from a long vacation away from your friends and have to tell them all about it. How would you excite your friends about all that you saw and did when you were away? You would probably show them pictures and videos of your trip and arrange them in a special way. Most meteorologists have special computers that they use in their forecast that show the viewers everything they have been studying before the forecast. Temperatures, cloud patterns, weather conditions, along with "movies" of satellite views of rain and snow, jet stream movements, and, of course, the all-important five- to seven-day forecast are all ready to be presented in an exciting "show" usually only a few minutes long!

Finally, it's time to actually do a weather forecast! After all of the preparations, most television meteorologists then stand in front of the "green screen" (see Chapter 6) and deliver a forecast to all of the people watching at home! If you look closely

1=A
2=C
3=D
4=E
5=G
6=H
7=I
8=L
9=N
10=O
11=P
12=R
13=S
14=T
15=U
16=W

Rainy Day Riddle

Two meteorologists are talking to each other. Use the decoder to fill in the puzzle grid and see how the conversation ends!

Why did you cut a hole in your new umbrella?

13	10		7		2	10	15	8	3
13	4	4		16	6	4	9		
7	14		13	14	10	11	11	4	3
12	1	7	9	7	9	5	!		

What's that thing in the weathercaster's ear?

During most weather forecasts on television, a person called a producer is often talking to the weathercaster through a tiny earpiece attached to the forecaster's ear. The producer tells the weather forecaster how much time is left and other important information the forecaster may need during the forecast. Now you know!

at most television weather forecasters, they are usually holding a remote controller (like the one you have for your TV) in their hands that controls their weather computer. When the right buttons are pressed, the weather maps from their computer change and move. What you don't see is often a small speaker that fits into their ear. With that, they can hear from the other people they work with that tell them how much time they have and how their weather forecast is going. Also, a small microphone is attached to the meteorologist's shirt so her voice can be heard load and clear through your television. From cameras and television monitors all over, green screens, microphones, remote controllers in their hands, directors and producers talking in their ear piece to the most important part—the weather forecast in their head—it's all part of a fun day at work for television meteorologists!

Freaky Forecast

Today has been a wacky weather day! Fill in the one letter that is missing from each sentence. Then see how quickly you can read this wild weather report.

__OUR __AST __RONTS __ROZE __LORIDA!

__EN __WISTERS __RASHED __EXAS __OWNS!

__ILD __INDS __REAKED __ISCONSIN __OODS!

__NCREDIBLE __CE __MMOBILIZED __DAHO!

FROM A WEATHER HOBBY TO A METEOROLOGIST

All right, you've got it, "the weather bug." Most meteorologists and weather enthusiasts will tell you they were first bitten by the "bug" when they were just children. The "bug" is a deep interest in weather—the science of weather, how it works, why it works, and how to better understand it! You know, all of the things you've been learning and reading about in this book. So what now? How can you take your interest in the science of weather and make it something more? Whether you want to become a meteorologist, a television weather forecaster, or someone who just loves to observe, record, and be a part of the atmosphere's daily motions, there's plenty you can do right now to get more involved. You can start by building a small home weather station and end up with a college degree in meteorology, broadcasting weather information to millions and millions of people!

One thing that all meteorologists do that you can start doing *right now* is simple weather observation. As a hobby, many weather enthusiasts record and write down how weather changes from day to day, or even hour to hour! It's fun, simple, and easy to do. Start a weather observation log book for each day by writing down sky conditions, cloud types, winds, temperatures, barometer readings, and precipitation. Using this book, you can make your own barometer (Chapter 2), build a rain gauge (Chapter 9), identify cloud types (Chapter 3), understand temperature and humidity readings (Chapter 2), and even read weather maps (Chapters 5 and 6). Following is a sample weather observation log. You can make your own, or copy the one in this book. It is important that you try your best to observe and record in your log book the weather at the same times each day, at least twice a day. Once you start recording and observing weather from your own special spot, it becomes a weather station. Yes, the beginning of your own backyard weather station. Now that's exciting!

SAMPLE WEATHER LOG

	MONDAY	TUESDAY	WEDNESDAY
	9 A.M./5 P.M.	9 A.M/6 P.M.	8 A.M./ 5:30 P.M.
Sky	cloudy/clear	clear/partly sunny	cloudy/cloudy
Cloud Type	stratus/none	none/cirrus	stratus/stratus
Temperature	63°/75°	55°/73°	53°/56°
Wind	north/north	south/light	windy south/ windy east
Barometer	30.25/30.23	30.10/30.00	29.95/29.90
Weather	rain/sunny	sunny/partly sunny	rain, windy/ still rainy

Sample weather log showing two observations each day. Some information you can get from your local news and weather report, like barometer and wind conditions.

Just like the toys and games you had when you were younger have changed as you grew, your weather observations and station will change over time, too. With the help from your family, you may be able to advance your weather hobby into something more. You may be able to buy some of your weather instruments. Many hardware stores and hobby shops sell barometers, rain gauges, wind instruments, and thermometer and humidity gauges. With more advanced weather equipment you can better observe and forecast weather changes from your home weather station. Your weather station can grow and change with you

Try This

WEATHER OBSERVING

Weather conditions like wind, temperature, sky conditions, barometer, and rainfall can all be recorded in your weather observation log book. Use your own weather instruments or even the reports given on television or on the Internet. Watch as conditions change from day to day and month to month. How long can you keep it going?

along with your interests and schooling. Many of the science classes you have in school will include weather-related topics and subjects. From there, your teachers, family members, and friends can help you expand your weather interests with the help of weather books, publications, and websites that include even more advanced weather maps, graphs, charts, images, and all sorts of meteorological information! Your weather station can grow and grow along with you!

Your weather hobby may end up taking up a big part of your life and even space! You may get to the point where there are weather instruments in your backyard, meteorology books all over your desk, weather maps on the wall, and daily observations taking place in the morning and evening. Some may even say it's more work than a fun hobby. But if you find yourself really enjoying everything about the science of weather, it's not work at all. It's a fun and interesting pastime. If you can take something that you feel is really fun and interesting and make a career out of it, you will love your job. Yes, your job. Someday you'll have a job and a career. If you do decide to go on to college and study meteorology, it's a lot of hard work and studying, but just like your home weather station, you'll be working at something you really like, so it'll seem like fun! So go ahead and watch cumulonimbus clouds develop into thunderstorms, track hurricanes in the Atlantic Ocean, and observe air pressure changing on your very own barometer. Meteorology is a very interesting and fun science, and you just might end up making a career out of it!

INTERVIEW A METEOROLOGIST

Write down ten good questions you'd like to ask a real meteorologist. Then, with the help of your parents, teachers, or family members, ask them to contact a meteorologist at a television station, college, or airport. Using e-mail, the phone, or by writing them a letter, see if the meteorologist will answer your questions. You may even end up meeting a meteorologist!

APPENDIX A
Resources

WEBSITES

The Weather Channel
Forecasts, weather maps, and everyday weather information for all ages!
www.weather.com

The Weather Dude
Great site for weather fun, music, articles, and information for kids.
www.wxdude.com

Weather Wiz Kids
This site is from a female meteorologist and offers many photos, art, weather folklore, and articles about the weather.
www.weatherwizkids.com

Hurricane Hunters
Interesting site with plenty of hurricane information and the missions of scientists who explore them with aircraft.
www.hurricanehunters.com

Snow Crystals
This is a fun and unique site full of information and pictures of snow crystals.
www.snowcrystals.com

Weather Instruments
This site has many different types and prices of weather equipment you can purchase.
www.weatherinstruments.com

BOOKS

Brotak, Edward. *Wild About Weather: 50 Wet, Windy & Wonderful Activities.* (Lark Books, 2005)

Cosgrove, Brian. *Weather.* (DK Eyewitness Books, DK Children, 2007)

De Paola, Tomie. *The Cloud Book.* (Holiday House, 1984)

Gibbons, Gail. *Planet Earth / Inside Out.* (Harper Trophy; New Edition, 1998)

Gibbons, Gail. *Weather Words and What They Mean.* (Holiday House, 1992)

Hiscock, Bruce. *The Big Storm.* (Atheneum Library Binding Edition, 1993)

Legault, Marie-Anne. *Scholastic Atlas of Weather.* (Scholastic Inc., 2004)

Mandell, Muriel. *Simple Weather Experiments with Everyday Materials.* (Sterling, Paperback Ed., 1991)

Shulman, Mark. *Wicked Weather.* (Discovery Channel, 2007)

Tocci, Salvatore. *Experiments with Weather.* (Children's Press, 2004)

APPENDIX B
Puzzle Answers

Watch the Weather • page 11

W H E N   S O U N D S
1 2 3   4 5
T R A V E L   F A R
6 7 8 9
A N D   W I D E ,   A
10 11 12 13
S T O R M Y   D A Y
14 15 16 17 18
W I L L   A R R I V E .
19 20   21 22 23

Places to
bake cakes
O V E N S
23 2 14

The opposite
of quiet
L O U D
8 15 4 12

Bend gently
back and forth
S W A Y
3 19 9 18

A bride's long
white headdress
V E I L
7 22 20

Prize given to
the winner
A W A R D
10 11 17 21 5

Adding and
subtracting
M A T H
16 13 6 1

Chit Chat • page 14

HOW DID YOU FIND THE WEATHER ON YOUR VACATION?

I JUST WENT OUTSIDE AND THERE IT WAS!

Sunny Sky, Cloudy Sky • page 18

Rhyme Time • page 24

IF CROWS FLY LOW, WINDS WILL BLOW. IF CROWS FLY HIGH, WINDS WILL DIE.

Many of these weather rhymes are loosely based on scientific fact. For example, when air pressure is high (during fair weather), it is easier for birds to fly at a high altitude. If air pressure is low (during bad weather), birds can't fly as high because the air is less dense.

High to Low • page 28

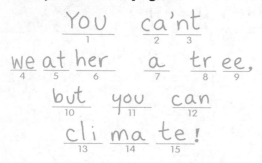

Blow Hard • page 31

W I N D   C A N   T U R N   T H E
BLADES   OF   HIGH-TECH
WIND   TURBINES   TO
MAKE   ELECTRICITY.

Wacky Weather • page 33

YOU   ca'nt
we at her   a   tr ee,
but   you   can
cli ma te!

The real answer: Climate is the
average weather conditions in an
area over a period of many years.

Listen Carefully • page 37

WHEN SOUNDS TRAVEL FAR AND WIDE, A STORMY DAY IT WILL BE OUTSIDE.

This saying is true! Sound travels better in air that is full of moisture than it does in dry air. That is why on a very overcast and humid day (the kind of weather you have just before a thunderstorm), you can hear a train whistle or highway noise that you usually don't notice!

Water Makes Weather • page 39

Wow! In deep water Kevin is now swimming!
I certainly hope this box fits under the bed.
Mimi stopped to see a cobra in Miami.
The cats were both under the house.
Two gruff ogres hum identical tunes.
Beth ails when she eats peanuts or milk.
The teacher was scolding Cedric loudly.
What a hassle! Ethan forget to pick me up!

Not Knot • page 41

What bow can't be tied?

A	R	K	Noah's boat
B	A	T	Baseball hitter
D	I	P	Quick swim
E	N	D	Not the start
E	B	B	Flow out
F	O	G	Very low cloud
O	W	L	Night bird

Follow the Arrows • page 44

START

ONE	WISPY	CIRRUS	CLO
IS	REI	NED	UDS
ARE	NICK	UP	AND
NAM	ED	MARE'S	THE
DO	INS	TAILS	OTH
WN	RA	ONE	ER

So True • page 54

World Weather • page 49

E L   T I E M P O (Spanish)

D A S   W E T T E R (German)

L E   T E M P S (French)

Smooth and Flat • page 56

To read this puzzle, you need to rotate the book a quarter turn counterclockwise. Then tilt the book away from you until it is almost level. Look across the letters as they stretch away from you to learn the name of the calm weather area near the equator.

THE DOLDRUMS

Slow Down! • page 65

M	C	O	G	H	U	H	G	N
G	T	H	A	C	H	I	C	H
N	H	G	H	S	H	C	G	H
G	W	G	C	H	A	R	H	C
H	C	M	G	B	H	O	C	D
I	H	E	H	C	S	C	O	G
C	G	C	F	G	H	W	G	C
G	A	C	T	C	E	C	H	R

MOUNTAINS

WARM BODIES
OF WATER

On Either Side • page 68

The greater the difference between the temperature and humidity, the more powerful the storm!

What Is a Derecho? • page 70

"DERECHO" IS THE SPANISH WORD FOR "STRAIGHT"

It's Simple • page 77

How can you use a rope to tell the weather?

H	A	N	G		I	T		O	U	T		T	H	E
W	I	N	D	O	W	.		I	F		T	H	E	
R	O	P	E		M	O	V	E	S	,		I	T	'	S
W	I	N	D	Y	.		I	F		I	T	'	S	
W	E	T	,		I	T	'	S		R	A	I	N	Y	!

Rain, Rain, Go Away • page 81

A SUN SHINY SHOWER WON'T LAST HALF AN HOUR.

Hink Pinks • page 83

1. Hole down which storm water flows
RAIN   DRAIN

2. White flakes that don't fall fast
SLOW   SNOW

3. Icy rain that falls in a tidy manner
NEAT   SLEET

4. Tropical weather event
WARM   STORM

5. Water vapor in the sky that makes thunder
LOUD   CLOUD

6. Friendly frozen water
NICE   ICE

7. Water vapor lying low over a swamp
BOG   FOG

Spin-n-Grin • page 89

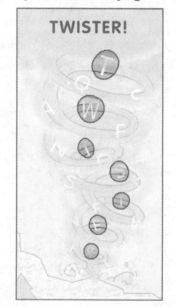

TWISTER!

Appendix B: Puzzle Answers

Watch Out! • page 91

What did the boy hurricane say to the girl hurricane?

LFX**I**X**F**X
LHXA**F**V
X**E**XM**F**X
YXL**E**FY**L**
EFL**O**FL**N**
YFXLF**O**F
FLX**U**XFL

ZAP ZAP ZAPPITY ZAP • page 97

Add up the number of...

...days in two years _730_

...sheets of paper in a ream _500_

...pennies in $10 _1,000_

...cookies in 20 dozen _240_

...toes on three people _30_

This is the total number of lightning strikes estimated in western Washington state during this one day! | 2,500 |

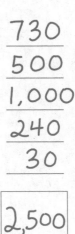

Snow Day • page 100

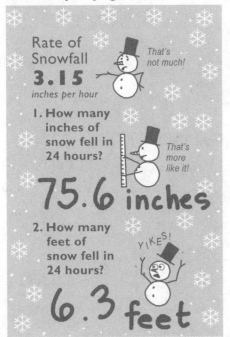

Rate of Snowfall **3.15** inches per hour

That's not much!

1. How many inches of snow fell in 24 hours?

That's more like it!

75.6 inches

2. How many feet of snow fell in 24 hours?

YIKES!

6.3 feet

Light Maze • page 104

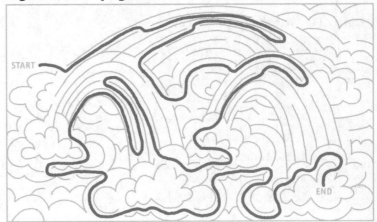

START

END

139

Bow Wow • page 107

Sky Lights • page 112

Jackpot • page 124

BECAUSE THE
METEOROLOGIST
PREDICTED
SOME CHANGE
IN THE
WEATHER!

Rainy Day Riddle • page 129

13	10		7		2	10	15	8	3
S	O		I		C	O	U	L	D

13	4	4		16	6	4	9		
S	E	E		W	H	E	N		

7	14		13	14	10	11	11	4	3
I	T		S	T	O	P	P	E	D

12	1	7	9	7	9	5			
R	A	I	N	I	N	G	!		

Freaky Forecast • page 130

Four Fast Fronts Froze Florida!

Ten Twisters Trashed Texas Towns!

Wild Winds Wreaked Wisconsin Woods!

Incredible Ice Imobilized Idaho!

Index